THE INFORMATION SUPERHIGHWAY

The Information Superhighway

Strategic Alliances in Telecommunications and Multimedia

Randall L. Carlson

St. Martin's Press
New York

HE
7568
.C37
1996

St. Martin's Press, Scholarly and Reference Division,
175 Fifth Avenue, New York, N.Y. 10010

First published in the United States of America in 1996

Printed in Great Britain

ISBN 0–312–16068–2

Library of Congress Cataloging-in-Publication Data
Carlson, Randall L.
The information superhighway : strategic alliances in
telecommunications and multimedia / Randall L. Carlson.
p.   cm.
Includes bibliographical references and index.
ISBN 0–312–16068–2
1. Information superhighway—Economic aspects.
2. Telecommunication—Economic aspects.   3. Strategic alliances
(Business)   4. Interactive multimedia—Economic aspects.   I. Title.
HE7568.C37   1996
384'.041—dc20   96–1323
                                                            CIP

To Dad and Mom

Contents

List of Figures

List of Tables

Acknowledgments

The research in this book stems from international business research conducted at the Fletcher School of Law and Diplomacy. The research was supported through the funding of the Fletcher School and the Nortel Corporation. Together these two institutions have made possible a much-needed study of strategic alliances in telecommunications and multimedia.

I would like to thank Professor Denis Simon for his guidance on the politics of alliances. Dr. Jim Doherty was particularly instrumental in data collection. I would also like to thank Professor Russ Neuman for his assistance on the methodological framework. Karen McMaster made it possible for these international persons to meet, making this work possible.

Nortel was very supportive of the work and contributed generously. I would like to thank Joao Mendonca, Pat Dowling, Jerry Aiken, Mark Starkebaum, Paul Brant, Alan Fraser, Larry Gaudet and Serge Fournier. Len Fawcett, Peter Knowles, and Gavin Alpe were instrumental in achieving the required Process Re-engineering research.

Neil Knight and Tom Bouchard of US West contributed generous amounts of time and materials for understanding the CATV–telco relationship.

I would like to thank all those who completed the questionnaires. For completing the first, very extensive questionnaire, I thank: Lotus Development Corp., Medrad Inc., Policy Management Systems Corp., Xilinx, Medicus Systems Corp., Merck & Co., and Honeywell Corp.

The author and publishers are grateful to Elsevier Science Limited, CMP Publications and the Institute for Management Science for permission to reproduce copyright material. Every effort has been made to contact all copyright-holders for permission to reproduce copyright material. If anything has been omitted, the publisher will be pleased to make the necessary arrangement at the earliest opportunity.

Last but not least, I thank Betsy Andrews for editorial saves, Macmillan and St. Martin's Press for publication, Keith Povey for edits and Rosabeth Moss Hunter for the book review.

RANDALL L. CARLSON

1 Introduction

The partnerships of the cable television, telephone and information services businesses will affect everyone interested in computers, the internet or movies. These companies have jumped on the partnership bandwagon in anticipation of a revolution in how we work and play. Cable companies are allying with long distance telephone companies and entertainment companies. Telephone companies partner with equipment suppliers and entertainment companies. Multimedia companies ally with everyone including museums, publishers, studios, and travel agents. Whatever the shape of these partnerships is, and however they evolve, the Information Superhighway will affect our work and play well into the next century.

The telephone companies (Bells) are shrugging off their utility mentality and developing entertainment programming portfolios necessary to compete in entertainment and information services. Cable companies are developing a high technical proficiency and are increasing investments in new technologies. Start-up companies are offering interactive games and virtual reality, and securing distribution through Bells and cable companies. The market is clearly evolving itself through alliances and according to Kanter, 'Giants are learning to dance.'[1]

Synergies developed across industries form a portfolio of strategic competencies. Individuals that promote synergies through cross-product teams, strategic alliances and mergers are highly valued in effecting corporate change. One Bell hired two vice presidents directly from Hollywood, a move unheard of five years ago. The utility culture would never have accepted the hiring of movie moguls into a telephone business. Now employees are aware how rapidly their businesses are changing and accept cross-organizational cooperation as a way of life. Employees realize that radical change must occur even if the benefits are not yet tangible.

The cable companies' alliance making is rooted in funding requirements. It costs each cable company upwards of $2000 for setting up one cable subscriber with set-top boxes and other interfaces. Cable companies can borrow funds only in relation to their subscriber base which is generally smaller than the Bells' bases. Cable companies form partnerships to increase the density and scope of subscribers in a particular geographic service region. An increased number of potential subscribers increases borrowing power.

In a similar competitive note, the telephone companies' lines on the telephone poles are of little use for the Information Superhighway. Going-it-alone, the Bells would have to totally revamp their infrastructure and install new lines on all telephone poles. Telephone companies partner with cable companies and share cable companies' lines that *are* suitable for the Information Superhighway. Additional partnerships with entertainment companies develop the competitive entertainment programming needed to attract cable television viewers.

1.1   THE TELECOMMUNICATIONS INDUSTRY

Until recently, telecommunications was a utility industry similar to power, transportation and the postal service. Telecommunications was mostly a voice service via telephone with some computer and data communications. Telecommunications companies were heavily regulated and strictly scrutinized by the Courts, the Federal Communications Commission (FCC) and Congress. Regulators maintained the American Telephone and Telegraph's (AT&T) monopoly to (i) realize universal service for all, (ii) increase reliability in tasks central to the public order and (iii) tap economies of scale and scope in services.[2] Regulators based their policy on the understanding that a 1% increase in telephones per capita could increase a nation's gross domestic product by 3%.[3] Through strict regulation of plain old telephone service (POTS), the US Bell System installed more telephones than any country in the world (114 million) and by 1990, there were 45.3 lines/100 inhabitants which exceeded the OECD average.[4] The national monopoly had almost achieved its goal of providing a basic telephone service to every American.

In 1984, the Justice Department found that the anti-competitive drawbacks of continuing the AT&T monopoly outweighed the monopoly advantages. It broke up the AT&T monopoly in 1984 and formed seven Regional Bell Operating Companies (RBOCs or Bells) with allotted geographical service regions. The Bells included Ameritech, Bell Atlantic, NYNEX, BellSouth, Pacific Bell, Southwestern Bell, US West. BellSouth received the greatest population in its region with 50 million people, Ameritech received 42 million and Bell Atlantic received 34 million.[5] The Bells were given a monopoly on local services within their region but were strictly barred from information services, cable television, manufacturing and non-telecommunications businesses. AT&T continued its monopoly on long-distance communications, equipment manufacturing and long-distance services.

1.2 ON RAMP TO THE INFORMATION SUPERHIGHWAY

New telecommunications services made possible through increased competition, less regulation and new technologies forced the Baby Bells (Bells) and cable television companies (cable) to reevaluate their competitive strategy. Bells and cable companies now see the strategic importance of services such as cable television, home shopping, cellular telephony, and high speed data services. They no longer ignore rising competition from sectors such as cable television and long distance that was previously monopolized.

The Bells are not satisfied with an assured monopoly in voice service as a quid-pro-quo for exclusion from other markets. Rural voice service had always been a bottleneck for AT&T and now is the only service monopoly that the Bells maintain. In the face of increased deregulation, the Baby Bells have become the subject of 'cherry picking.' New service providers 'cherry pick' the best metropolitan opportunities and leave rural customers alone. The Bells are fighting back and exchanging their monopoly position for decreased regulation in other services.

The cultural and strategic changes needed to address these new challenges were at first impeded by the old utility mentality. The Bells set up fully-owned subsidiaries to address new services such as cellular, business, information, consumer, pay phone, and long distance. Unfortunately, most new businesses offered little self-sufficiency and were financially reliant on their mother companies.

Today, the unifying strategic goal of telephone companies' business units is to increase traffic on the mother company's network. For example, the cellular business unit directs all traffic from cellular systems through cellular base stations and onto the existing terrestrial Public Switched Telephone Network (PSTN). The cellular business unit collects its revenues based on billing generated by the cellular network. The mother company then collects its revenues for cellular traffic passing through the PSTN.

1.3 THE BELLS' NEW SERVICES STRATEGY

Cable television services have long been the lure of the Bells. It is generally considered that the holder of the content is the holder of the control. Whoever can control what goes on the lines, will control what is done with that information. An incredible amount of control and

persuasion is effected through new services that subscribers relate to and enjoy. For example, a customer will complain loudly if his or her favorite programme is not carried by a service provider. If there is an option, that subscriber might change to another service provider that carries the programme.

In bringing more entertainment content onto their network, telephone companies have begun a serious initiative to form partnerships with entertainment companies. The Bells leave content provision to partners, whether that partner is a cable, movie or broadcasting company. Through partnerships, the Bells are facilitating the Information Superhighway in the most efficient way possible.

The non-content strategy of the Bells empowers the end-user into generating content. Services such as telecommuting, videoconferencing, and virtual reality allow end-users to generate content that would never have existed before. For example, communities that now have town meetings using video conferencing systems generate billable traffic that had never existed. In the past, town hall meeting benefited auto makers, gas and heating companies. By introducing new services, telephone companies are capturing a small portion of every content-generating activity.

There is a need for many content-generating services but the relative success of each service is only known after it is tested and introduced. Will there really be a shift towards telecommuting? Will the savings of gasoline, pollution, and time outweigh the social and economic synergies of meeting in a town hall? Will the availability of videoconferencing actually increase democracy and community consensus-building? Only though joint testing, trials, and development, can the potential of these markets be feasibly measured.

1.4 REASONS FOR ALLIANCES

A survey of 90 telecommunications companies determined the top reasons for forming alliances on the Information Superhighway (a complete discussion of the survey is found in Chapter 14). In response, 28% of all respondents (see Figure 1.1) chose 'Sharing of financial risk and rewards' as the leading reason to form alliances. Sharing of financial risk included such factors as *increase revenues, share risk/reward, reduce development costs, mitigate risk* and *increase profitability*. A further 21% of respondents chose 'exchange of technical info/know-how.' These factors included *access to new technology/skills, increase R&D capa-*

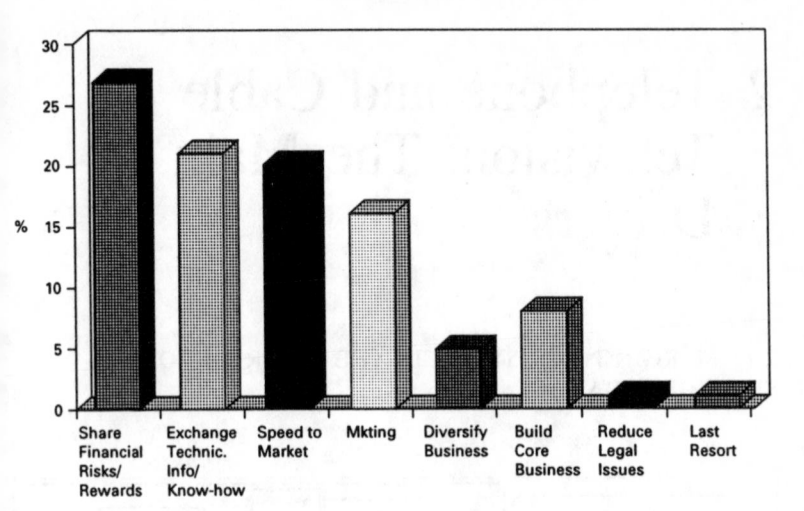

Figure 1.1   Top Motivations for Forming Alliances

bility, technological/product leverage and *access unique capability of partner.* 'Organizational efficiency' was chosen by 20% of respondents as a main motivational factor in forming alliances. This included factors such as *reduce time to market, expedite product to marketplace, expedience* and *save development time.* 'Marketing' factors was the top motivation for alliances 16% of the time. Marketing factors included, *access partner's distribution system, better position of partner in target market, gain partner's reputation* and *access new market.*

Alliances are actively used to mitigate high entry fees, adapt to rapidly changing regulations and develop consolidated technologies. The data explaining the reasons for alliances matches the demands of the marketplace and points to a viable source of competitive advantage. The competitive demands of the Information Superhighway have put alliances to the test as the main means of evolving an industry. This book should add to our understanding of alliances as important business instruments.

2 Telephone and Cable Television: The Main Drivers

2.1 MERGING INDUSTRIES IN THE INFORMATION SUPERHIGHWAY

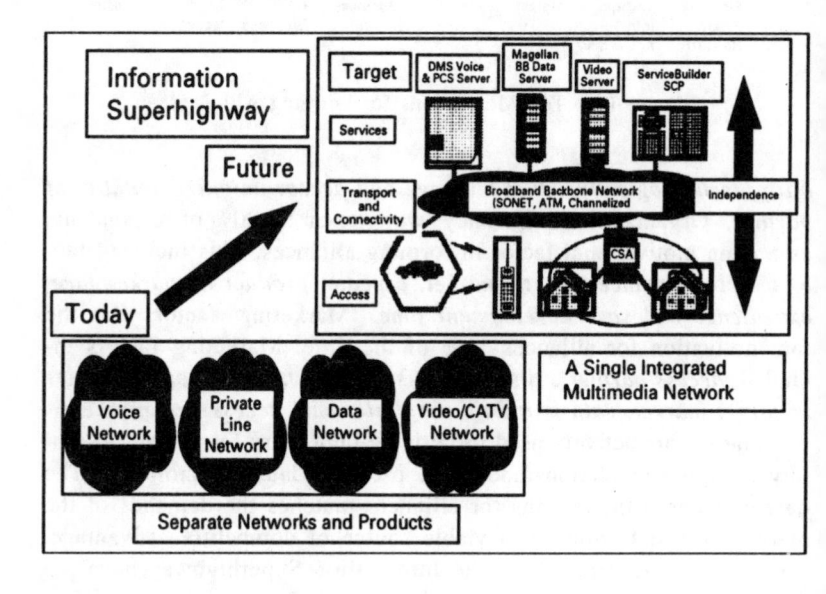

Figure 2.1   The Information Superhighway

Telephone and cable television (Community Antenna Television Service: CATV) are merging along with respective technologies in voice, data and video (see Figure 2.1). Through the integration of separate networks and products, a single integrated multimedia network (the Information Superhighway) is being developed. Information Superhighway services are now available in many homes and businesses wired for both telephone and cable television. Consumers will choose between

the cable or telephone company for integrated cable and telephone services. Instead of receiving cable television from the CATV company and telephone from the telephone company, both are provided by each company. The combination of both existing and planned facilities is the foundation of the National Information Infrastructure (NII), the technological infrastructure for new services.

As new services become available, the single point of contact, i.e. telephone or CATV company allows easy access to the Information Superhighway. The actual services and content that a consumer chooses from the home are purchased directly from their service provider. For example, a Distance Learning programme that facilitates University Degrees via videoconferencing can bill students through the telephone company. The telephone company (Bell) will provide the transmission facility for the videoconferencing and pay the university royalties on information content. This is more efficient than having a separate transmission facility set up by the university that spans the entire country and bills the student directly. Instead, subscribers purchase university degree courses through telephone or cable companies and pay the charges through existing billing procedures. By integrating a wide array of services in a programming portfolio, customers can choose from a large selection of Information Superhighway services with relative ease.

As shown in Figure 2.2, communications, entertainment and information technologies overlap in many areas. The true merger of communications, entertainment and information makes new services possible, e.g. workgroup collaboration, distance learning, news retrieval, on-line encyclopedias, interactive games, etc. The key concepts in the evolution of these technologies are: (i) voice services to be provided through cable television lines, (ii) cable services to be provided through telephone lines, and (iii) interactive services. By merging the technologies, a more widespread distribution of new services is economically feasible.

The Information Superhighway will require a number of new devices that can handle the combination of voice, data and user interaction. The set-top multimedia computer will be an important device that acts as a sophisticated cable TV box. For example, when a television talk show host asks viewers to call in and voice their opinions, viewers now use their telephone. New systems will use an interactive set-top multimedia computer and the viewer will no longer have to use the telephone as a separate device. Multimedia computers allow the viewer to speak, press response buttons, and participate in talk shows. The computer integrates point of sales functionality that allows users to

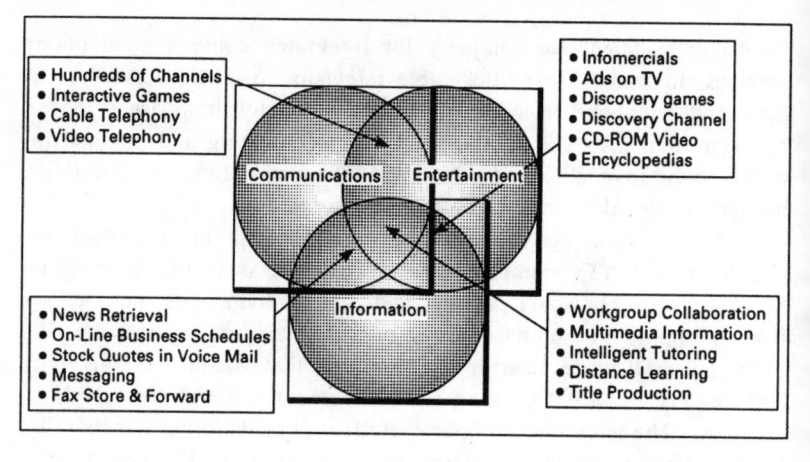

- Hundreds of Channels
- Interactive Games
- Cable Telephony
- Video Telephony

- Infomercials
- Ads on TV
- Discovery games
- Discovery Channel
- CD-ROM Video
- Encyclopedias

Communications   Entertainment

- News Retrieval
- On-Line Business Schedules
- Stock Quotes in Voice Mail
- Messaging
- Fax Store & Forward

Information

- Workgroup Collaboration
- Multimedia Information
- Intelligent Tutoring
- Distance Learning
- Title Production

Source: 'Multimedia Services and Technology: Opportunities and Partnerships' (Englewood, CO: US West Multimedia Communications, Inc., October 26, 1993, 2).

Figure 2.2   Merging Communications, Information and Entertainment
Applications and Technology

purchase items directly from their home. The purchaser simply slides a credit card through a multimedia computer, gives authorization for the charges and transfers the receipt into an accounting database. Next day deliveries distribute the goods promptly to viewers. All services will be combined and users may get a sense of virtual reality, i.e. of 'actually having gone shopping', etc.

2.2   COMPANY STRATEGY

From the Bells' perspective, the main revenue driving factor for the short term is to integrate CATV and telephone service. Investments required for plain old telephone service (POTS) over cable plant typically range from $750 to $900 per subscriber. The Bells want to maximize their telephone subscribers both in-region and out-of-region since voice is still profitable. As new products are developed that take advantage of integrated voice and video, the Bells will find in-region partners to position themselves in entertainment. As new enhanced services arrive, POTS will become just another service included in an Information Superhighway programming portfolio.

From a cable company's perspective, it must penetrate the $100 billion telephony market to stay competitive. Rate cuts imposed on cable companies after the 1992 Cable Act have cut into profit margins needed for new investments. In addition, the Bells entering into CATV may take market share away from cable companies. Cable companies must now penetrate telephone markets to increase their revenue base. A cable company's strategy includes forming strategic alliances with Interexchange Carriers (IXC) and out-of-region Local Exchange Carriers (LEC), electric utilities, and other CATV companies. For example, the WirelessCo alliance for delivering global voice and entertainment services is composed of Cox (CATV), Comcast (CATV), TCI (CATV) and Sprint (IXC).

Creating new CATV technologies is a complex and expensive undertaking. The estimated cost per multimedia subscriber averages $2160–$2900. Banks will lend CATV companies only $1000–$1100 per subscriber.[1] In 7–8 years, the cable industry expects to penetrate 30% of voice telephony, 20% of high-speed data and 5% of video telephony.[2] In comparison, deregulated cable companies in the United Kingdom have achieved 25–26% penetration in voice telephony. Since most cable TV companies are fully leveraged, the cost of developing new technologies must be leveraged through partnerships.

Fueling cable television's R&D and purchasing efforts is an alliance of cable companies called CableLabs. CableLabs' mission is to develop next generation cable telephony equipment. The best R&D teams for addressing multimedia products are composed of members from relevant industries, i.e. CATV, telephony and entertainment. Assembling diverse teams and getting them to speak in confidence requires alliances like CableLabs. It must purchase $2 billion in switching equipment to penetrate only 2% of the voice market.

By partnering with overlapping companies, greater penetration of a single geographic area achieves better cash flow from existing systems. Clustering cuts the cost per subscriber since existing cable systems are better utilized. Sharing programming content with alliance partners creates economies of scale by distributing shows to more viewers. Since cable companies are highly leveraged, alliances form a critical strategy for increasing efficiency, borrowing power, and competitiveness.

2.3 CATV–TELEPHONE TECHNOLOGY

Communications, entertainment, and information industries are merging due to the convergence of technologies and the demand of consumers

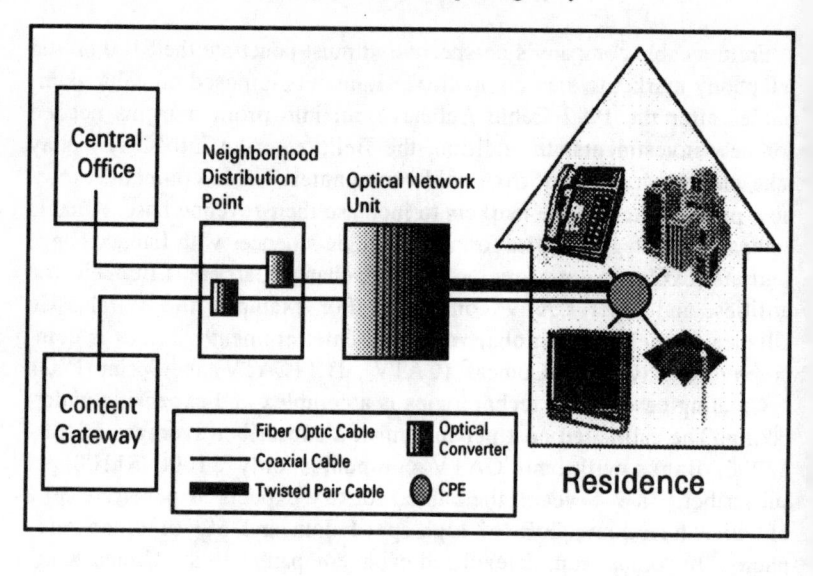

Figure 2.3   How Broadband Works

who want everything-in-one. It is really the merged technologies that make it possible for consumers to have a unified solution. Products are driving the standards rather than technical standards driving products, as was the traditional case. Alliances accelerate new unified products to market and drive legislation, bringing multimedia products into wider acceptance.

Initially, the Bells companies are disadvantaged because of outdated cables on the telephone poles. Most Bells have existing cable specifically designed for an older generation of switching technology. Telephone company cables are filled with thousands of wire pairs, each capable of carrying only one conversation. When you needed to carry more conversations, common practice dictated simply increasing the number of cable pairs. Older central office switches had one termination unit for each pair entering the office and would switch calls out to the appropriate pair servicing the called destination. New digital switches discern multiple conversations on one coaxial or fiber optic cable, hence the importance of increasing the quality of one cable rather than increasing the number of cables. Exist-ing telephone cables containing thousands of pairs in each cable are of little use for Information Superhighway systems.

The cable television cable on those same poles uses only one co-

axial cable that is capable of carrying Information Superhighway services. Coaxial cable has a high bandwidth (ability to carry information). Through multiplexing technology, one coaxial cable can carry hundreds of conversations and programmes simultaneously. It can also carry between 62 and 78 television channels. Conversely, one telephone pair cannot carry even one channel. Advancements in technology will make coaxial cable fully acceptable for transporting voice, data and video. Cable companies are thus better positioned to accept new multimedia products onto their coaxial infrastructure as compared with the Bells' existing infrastructure.

An explanation of the technical convergence of cable television and telephone technologies to the home is shown in Figure 2.3. Figure 2.3 demonstrates how technologies from different industries are merging. The Central Office (CO) is owned by the telephone company for voice communications services. The Content Gateway provides cable television and is controlled by the CATV companies. The Optical Network Unit is where the telephone and cable lines meet and join the two services. Services are transmitted into the home by twisted pair cable for telephony, and by coaxial cable for standard video offerings and interactive services. The residence has Customer Premises Equipment (CPE) which distributes and unscrambles services such as telephony, home shopping, entertainment and distance learning.

Later versions of the technology will actually switch the channel at the Content Gateway, thereby decreasing the bandwidth requirement for cable television. When customers switch channels on their TV set, the channel is actually being switched at a central site and only that one channel is being transmitted to their home. In the past, all channels were transmitted to the home and the viewer changed channels locally. By transmitting only one channel at a time, bandwidth is freed-up for other services such as telephony, data transmission, and video.

The beauty of integrating cable television and telephony is that all transmission requirements can be divided among existing physical lines. Alliance partners can develop enhanced services using existing facilities without installing completely new fiber cables. Eventually, voice and data will be carried from the Neighborhood Distribution Point to the home via one fiber cable. Who will own and install each cable is a major issue that will be played out by alliance partners.

2.4   CATV–TELCO REGULATIONS

200 000 lawyers, lobbyists an associated employees ply their trade here . . . the conclusion of the journey to competition will not be easy (FCC Chairman Reed Hunt).

I worry about how the cable operators are going to successfully make a transition. I worry about phone companies with vastly greater resources, particularly now that cable's been to some degree crippled. We were already smaller than the phone companies, and if there is an all-out competition, you're smaller to start with and you've been crippled (Ted Turner, commenting on prospects for the Turner – TCI – Time Warner venture).

Some of the barriers to telecom service market entry have to be handled very delicately because they are difficult, Vice President Al Gore, commenting on passage of the 1995 Communications Act.

2.4.1   The CATV–Telco Cross-ownership Ban

Evolution of Regulation

Strategic alliances have always been important to telephone companies since Community Antenna Television Service (CATV) first started. CATV began when communities erected large antennas for better television reception and transported the signal by putting up lines on telephone poles. Telephone companies allowed cable to be placed on their poles as long as the CATV company was affiliated or partially owned by them. Since most telephone companies were searching for a way to develop new services, cable television was a natural partner. When the Federal government disallowed any cross-ownership between cable and telephone companies through a cable–telco cross-ownership ban, cable companies continued to string up their cables.

Since the cable that CATV companies have is more effective for the Information Superhighway than telephone cable, telephone companies recognize a potential disaster. New services by CATV companies could be potentially activated with the flip of a switch. The telephone companies face the risk of being handicapped by outdated cable systems. The Bells can only justify expensive cable upgrades necessary for the Information Superhighway if the Federal Government allows free entry into CATV. In order to set the stage for regulatory changes, the Bells

proved that cable companies had a near monopoly-hold on cable television. A brief history of the relevant regulatory changes follows.

In 1968, a Federal Communications Commission (FCC) study revealed varying degrees of ownership (essentially strategic alliances) between telephone companies and CATV companies.[3] The first recognition that telephone companies had an unfair advantage because of telephone pole ownership can be found in the FCC's 1970 Order.[4] It states, 'The monopoly position of the telephone company in the community [results in] effective control of the pole.' In 1978, Congress passed the Pole Attachment Act which authorized the FCC to 'regulate the rates, terms, and conditions for pole attachments'.[5] In addition, telephone companies were required to lease-out a certain percentage of their 'video transport' capacity. The regulation precluded telephone companies and cable affiliates from monopolizing existing and future lines on telephone poles.

In the early 1980s, the FCC began a policy called the CATV–telco cross-ownership ban that prohibited cross-ownership between telephone companies and CATV companies. In November, 1981, the FCC's so-called OPP Report[6] advised that the CATV–telco cross-ownership restrictions 'must be retained.' The FCC was concerned about cross-subsidization, protection of an infant (CATV) industry, and promoting free access to poles.

In 1984, the FCC passed the 1984 Communications Policy Act[7] (the 1984 Cable Act) containing the famous Section 533(b) telco–CATV cross-ownership ban (see the full text of Section 533 in Appendix 2). Section 533(b) made it illegal for telephone companies to have any ownership of CATV operators in their region. In the early 1990s, the economic sensibility of strategic alliances led the FCC to reexamine the 1984 Act. In August, 1992, the FCC recommended to Congress 'that it amend the Cable Act to permit the local telephone companies to provide video programming directly to subscribers in their telephone service areas, subject to appropriate safeguards'.[8] The Commission concluded that,

the risks of anticompetitive conduct by the local telephone companies in connection with the direct provision of video programming have been attenuated by the enormous growth of the cable industry with the result that any remaining risk of anticompetitive conduct by the local telephone companies is outweighed by the public interest benefits their entry would bring.[9]

Elimination of the Cable Act restriction would increase competition in the video marketplace, spurring investment necessary to deploy an advanced infrastructure and increase the diversity of services available to the public.[10]

Prevention of cross-subsidization had always been a main justification for continuing the CATV–telco cross-ownership ban. Because CATV and telephone companies share some fixed costs, it is often difficult to discover cross-subsidization by source costing. Monitoring cross-subsidization is troublesome when facilities such as poles, cables and switches are shared. Cross-ownership and therefore cross-subsidization allow a telephone company to show losses on its telephone business and profits on its CATV business. Losses on telephone businesses provide justification to the Department of Public Utilities (DPUC) for monopoly rate increases. The telephone operator can then transfer investments into cable TV businesses. Telephone rate bases would be increased and telephone customers might pay for cable TV services that were unnecessary as a basic service.

The CATV industry has grown tremendously since the origination of CATV–telco legislation in 1970 and Congress is reconsidering present legislation. In 1970, there was only 9% availability of CATV to US homes versus 96% in 1993.[11] In 1970, total CATV industry revenues were $345 million versus $21 billion in 1992.[12] The five largest cable operators served 40% of all subscribers and had virtual monopoly status in all areas. While the FCC and the Department of Justice supported overturning the CATV–telco cross-ownership ban, the Senate found the cross-ownership ban an enhancement to competition. Since 1989, six separate bills have considered lifting the ban but Congress never acted to eliminate the *de facto* monopoly of CATV providers. In 1992, Congress increased regulation of CATV in the 1992 Cable Television Consumer Protection and Competition Act.

Moving Towards Deregulation

FCC studies show that in only 1% of service areas is there any competition in cable television and in those 1% of areas, basic cable rates are often lower. Telephone companies have proved beyond reasonable doubt that cable television was a *de facto* monopoly and was providing services that were increasingly important to the average consumer. Through cable television, cable subscribers could not only watch television but also shop, study for college degrees, get involved in local

activities, and order televized major sports events. The relevance of these services to average households could no longer be considered as simple as watching television. Nearly 60% of US households had cable television in 1994 and these households would clearly not benefit from a continued monopoly on cable service. Telephone companies recognized that cable television's monopoly on service had to be broken and that they must be allowed to provide additional services.

The following two regulatory ideas have served to reduce or eliminate the CATV–telco cross-ownership ban: (i) the House of Representatives wanted to preserve diversity of ownership of media outlets since the consumer is expected to benefit when a diversity of ownership exists *vis-à-vis* monopolization, and (ii) despite the ban on telephone companies from owning cable companies and vice-versa, telephone companies can now provide 'video transport.' In other words, telephone companies can offer a leased-line service to a CATV operator. The CATV operator puts the video programming on the telephone lines and the set-top termination equipment at the customer site. The telephone company has no involvement in 'video programming' but can 'transport' video.

In 1993, Bell Atlantic subsidiaries Chesapeake and Potomac Telephone Company of Virginia and Bell Atlantic Video Services challenged the First Amendment Constitutionality of the 1984 Cable Act. The US District Court found the CATV–telco cross-ownership ban to be 'unconstitutional as a violation of plaintiffs' First Amendment Right to free expression.[13] The court found that the complete ban on telephone companies from video programming restricted Free Speech rights more than was necessary to further the government's legitimate interests. The US government can only enact regulation that may not burden substantially more speech than is necessary to further the government's legitimate interests.[14] The regulation must promote a substantial government interest that would be achieved less effectively without the regulation.[15] The court found that there exists a range of alternatives with substantially less restriction on Free Speech than a complete ban on telephone companies from the cable industry. The Court ruled for the plaintiffs and additional rulings have also brought the repeal of the cross-ownership ban for various telephone companies.

In 1994–1995, the regulatory structure of telecommunications and cable television was relaxed further due to: (i) the Bells' commitments to Vice President Al Gore's Information Superhighway hinging on entrance into cable television and information services; (ii) multiple rulings favoring the elimination of the CATV–telco cross-ownership

ban; (iii) the merging of voice, video and information technologies; and (iv) Congress acting on the 1995 Telecommunications Bill.

The Existing Balance

The Bells have now targeted the $23 billion US CATV market and cable operators are targeting the $65 billion long-distance telecommunications market.[16] In return for their newly-won freedoms, companies will forfeit monopoly status in various service fiefdoms.

It appears that the Bells have initially gained an upper hand over cable TV competitors in the race for the Information Highway. The 1992 Cable Act, passed by Congress on October 5, 1992, introduced rate regulation on cable companies. Previously, there was virtually no rate regulation for cable television. The 1992 Cable Act required cable companies to reduce their rates by as much as 17% on basic programming.[17] Increases in cable rates could not exceed an inflation indexed amount, plus increases in certain costs that were beyond the cable operator's control. The 1992 Cable Act also introduced regulation in franchising, local station broadcasts and ownership in competing services. The Cable Act was similar to legislation governing Bells' monopoly control over local telephone service. Cable companies were found to have a national oligopolistic hold on the market with *de facto* monopolies in service regions. They were regulated to keep a base cable television service affordable as a 'universal service'.

While the cable companies have initially been hit the hardest by the legislation, deregulation is easing their woes. In June 1995, the Senate approved legislation which rescinds many price controls of the Cable Act. The legislation lifts the CATV–telco cross-ownership ban so the local infrastructure investments are made by those with the biggest pockets. Service providers are re-evaluating their competitive positions, redirecting R&D, and accelerating service deployment using all 'friendly' infrastructure.

2.4.2 Line of Business Restrictions

Before the 1984 breakup of AT&T, Western Electric was the sole manufacturing arm of AT&T. It has been speculated, although never proven, that AT&T cross-subsidized equipment manufacture from local exchange services. In certain situations, AT&T might have used cross-subsidization to price new competitors out of the market. The Bells were fully-controlled subsidiaries of AT&T and were in some

ways obligated to purchase equipment from Western Electric. The Bells gave AT&T and Bell Labs access to information needed for R&D and competitive tenders. Until 1984, AT&T sold over 80% of all US telecommunications equipment.

After the breakup, AT&T lost its 22 subsidiaries but retained its long-distance services and equipment manufacturing operations. Local exchange service, the 'bottleneck' of their business, was given to the newly independent Bells. Each Bell had a monopoly to provide service within one region (e.g. local exchange for NYNEX: New York, Rhode Island, Massachusetts, New Hampshire, Maine and Vermont) but was subject to the line of business restrictions.

The line of business restrictions disallowed Bells from manufacturing their own equipment, providing information services, competing in non-telecommunications businesses, and providing interexchange service. In manufacturing, Bells were also allowed to provide but not manufacture Customer Premises Equipment (CPE). CPE is used by large customers for internal [Centrex] switching. Bells were also allowed to produce, publish, and distribute the 'Yellow Pages' but not publish in general. Bells were to be regulated as monopolies so they would not abuse their monopoly status.

The line of business restrictions were deemed necessary because of (i) discriminatory practices and (ii) the local exchange monopoly. Policy makers were aware of how monopolies could disadvantage new competitors breaking into controlled markets. It is common for a monopolist to offer little access to facilities, provide low quality facilities, and delay responses. A monopoly provider can attempt to stave off interexchange carriers (carriers which service between regions of Bells such as AT&T, MCI and Sprint) by providing inferior quality and expensive local lines. Bells were given the local exchange monopoly with the inherent danger of cross-subsidization into other businesses. Although the new Bells were considered regional monopolies and easier to oversee than the entire Bell System, regulators found it impossible to oversee all their business dealings.

From the outset in 1984, the line of business restrictions were not meant to be permanent and provisions were made for their removal. If the Bells could petition the Court and show they would not abuse monopoly power in a new market, the restrictions might be lifted. The Triennial Review procedure was established so that the Department of Justice could report to the Court every three years concerning the continued need for the line of business restrictions. The first Triennial Review occurred in 1987 and the Department of Justice's Huber Report

recommended the complete removal of the manufacturing, non-telecommunications, information restrictions, and modification of the long-distance service restrictions. The Department of Justice then asked the court for a complete removal of the line of business restrictions, except for long-distance services. The seven Bells, AT&T, and the FCC testified and petitioned for removal of the restrictions. The Court ruled to remove the non-telecommunications business restrictions but left the others intact. Bells would be allowed to operate separate businesses in separate subsidiaries, whose total net revenues were limited to 10% of the mother Bell's total net revenues.[18] The primary concern was that the non-telecommunications business might be cross-subsidized from monopoly revenue.

The information services line of business restriction was strongly contested in the Triennial Review because of the profitability of information-based businesses. Telephone companies already possessed the perfect distribution systems for information services through their telephone lines. Section IV(J) of the 1982 Consent Decree defined information services as, 'the offering of a capability for generating, acquiring, storing, transforming, processing, retrieving, utilizing, or making available information which may be conveyed via telecommunications.'[19] The court found information services vulnerable to manipulation and discrimination in access or transmission quality. It seemed easy for the Bells to use their monopolies anti-competitively if they entered the market.[20]

In 1987, the information services restriction was reduced to the extent that Bells could provide information services generated by others.[21] There were obvious economic and social advantages to the impartial provision of information and the telephone system was one of the few means for widespread interactive communications. However, the Bells, would not, in any way, be allowed to compete with the information providers. Finally, in 1993, the Court ruled to remove information services from the line of business restrictions due to the increasing competition of AT&T, IBM, GE and others in information businesses.[22] Removal of the restrictions was critical to the full multimedia evolution of the Information Superhighway.

The manufacture of CPE is an area being strongly considered for deregulation, especially considering the large investments the Bells have made in R&D. Bellcore, the joint R&D consortium founded by the Bells after divestiture, is struggling for identity and wants to manufacture. The Independent Data Communications Manufacturers Association (IDCMA) opposes lifting of the restrictions and asserts that Bells

still have monopoly advantages. IDCMA asserts that Bells would favor their own CPE equipment through cross-subsidization, discrimination, bundling and other anti-competitive policies.[23] IDCMA cited 'repeated instances of anticompetitive conduct during the last ten years – in CPE provision, telecommunications equipment procurement, enhanced services, and inside wiring'.[24]

Eventually the line of business restrictions may be repealed, allowing more open competition. The Information Superhighway requires equipment and service to be provided by overlapping companies and partners. In order to realize the corporate commitments to infrastructure and R&D necessary for the Information Superhighway, regulators are taking a more hands-off approach.

3 US West's Full Service Network[1]

3.1 WEST'S PERSPECTIVE

US West, a 14-state Regional Bell Operating Company, has always used alliances in the pursuit of its multimedia strategy. In 1988, US West entered the UK market by acquiring a minority interest in Cable London. This was the first time that a telephone company had bought-into a cable television company in the UK. US West foresaw changes in regulations and was intent on offering plain old telephone service (POTS) through a cable television partner's lines.

In December 1991, US West and Telecommunications International (TCI) merged their UK properties in a joint venture called TeleWest. TeleWest was one of the first companies to offer both cable and phone service in a deregulated UK market. TeleWest serves 252 000 cable customers and has 182 000 telephone lines.[2] It also provides a testbed for services that will be introduced in a deregulated US market.

In June 1992, AT&T, US West, Time Warner Entertainment (TWE) and TCI began a joint trial of Viewer-controlled Cable Television (VCTV) which allowed customers in Orlando, Florida to request any movie at any time. Customers didn't need to check programme listings and showing times. They would simply call-in, ask for a movie, and an attendant would manually insert a video tape into a VCR player and transmit the movie to the caller's TV set.

The original VCTV trial focused primarily on measuring the market size for viewers calling in for any movie at any time. The results showed that customers wanted more that just movies. In fact, some viewers did not mind waiting for movie start times since a meeting of family or friends was the focal point of an evening's entertainment. Time Warner found other services increasing in both popularity and profitability, e.g. home shopping, information services, and interactive video games (see Figure 3.1). One service in particular, home shopping, is extremely profitable and Forbes expects it to capture between 5% and 15% of the $2.1 trillion US retail market. Within a decade, analyst Steven Kernkraut predicts sales of $100 billion.[3]

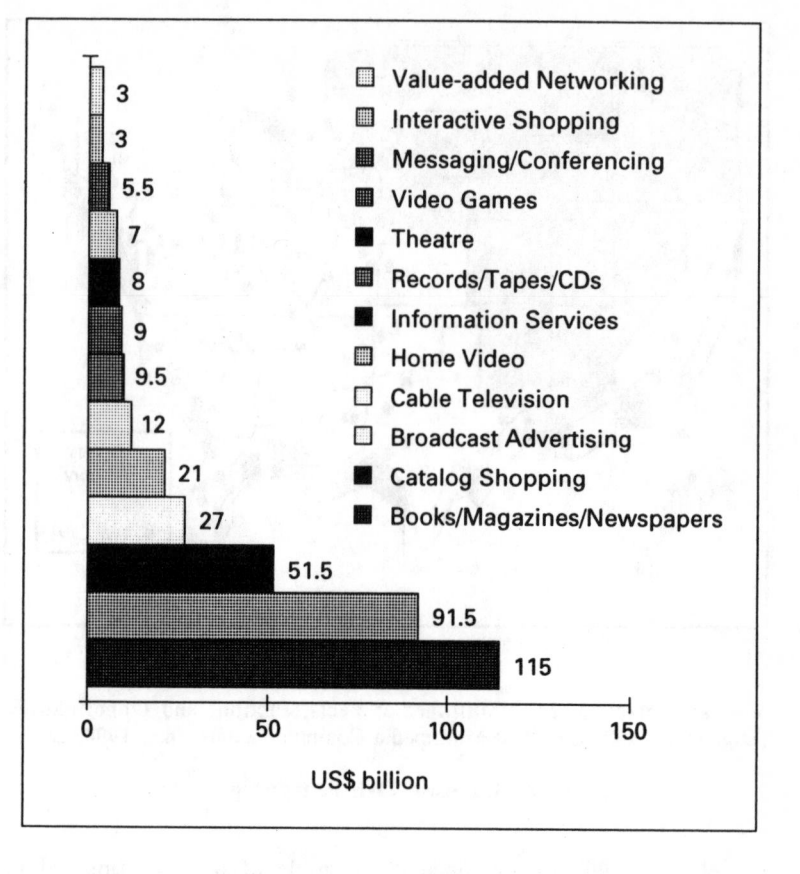

Source: Bear Stearns, Salomon Brothers (1994).

Figure 3.1   Current Home Entertainment Market

One home shopping service is the Automall program that displays full graphics and statistics on cars and trucks. If the customer is interested, a salesman drives the car or truck to the viewer's home for a test drive.[4] The customer can purchase the vehicle outright without ever stepping into the dealer's showroom.

Results of the VCTV trial are guiding Time Warner's service deployment strategy for its Full Service Network. The Full Service Network integrates voice, video and data and offers a highly profitable portfolio of services that also includes movies.

In 1993, US West decided that interactive video, information and communications services were vital to its long-term strategy. It acted

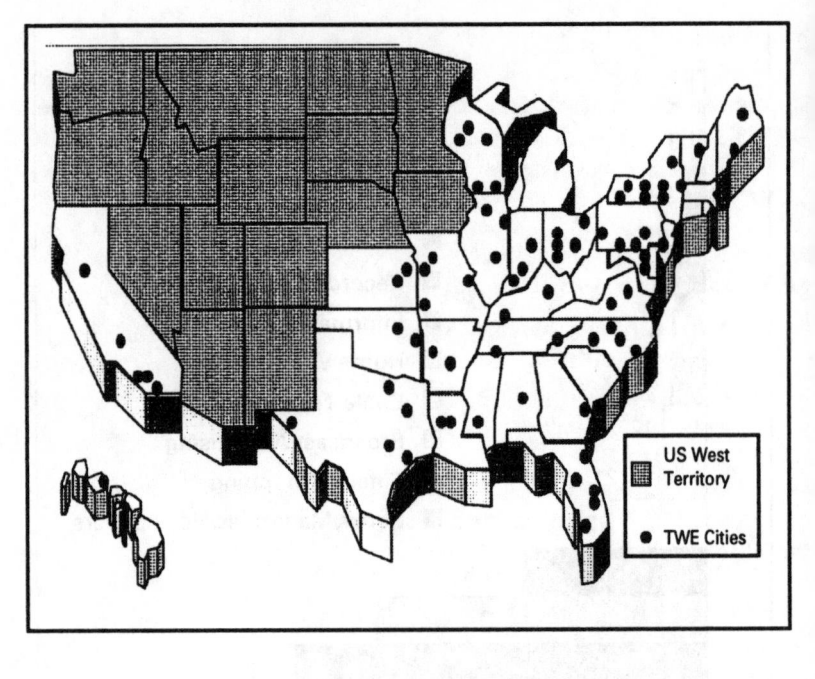

Source: Wetzel, J. M., 'Multimedia: Facts, Fiction, and Opportunities' (Englewood, CO: US West Multimedia Communications, Inc., 1994, 2).

Figure 3.2   US West–TWE Partnership Presence

in February 1993 to announce the upgrade of large portions of its network for accommodating Full Service Network applications. US West had long before set its sights on the in-region area (the regulated 14-state operating region), out-of-region (the other 36 states) and international (the rest of world). But US West could only perform upgrades within the in-region area.

To capture the out-of-region market, US West invested $2.5 billion for a 25.51% interest in Time Warner Entertainment. The first major goal of the alliance was to upgrade major portions of the combined networks. This was a strategic alliance that would speed the development of Full Service Networks in out-of-region areas. As shown in Figure 3.2, Time Warner Entertainment provided extensive coverage in major metropolitan districts out-of-region.[5] Fortunately, there was little overlap of TWE's properties with US West's service region which would have to be divested after the alliance.

US West–TWE is an alliance of strategy in that it is driven by US West's mission of becoming a global multimedia company. According to the Modified Final Judgment (MFJ), Bells are not allowed to offer POTS service in areas outside of their MFJ-designated region. While Bells cannot provide voice service in out-of-region local exchange carrier (LEC) areas, they can provide cable television.

In the Time Warner alliance, US West's economic modeling of the investment included:

- *Current operation*: revenue potential of 7.1 million subscribers + operations in 24 of the top 50 Metropolitan Service Areas + two-thirds of market share in >100 000 subscribers/cluster – divestiture required from 85 000 subscribers located in US West's region (due to the MFJ).
- *POTS investment*: cost to upgrade and install telephone switches and to offer POTS over existing CATV facilities.
- *Multimedia investment*: upgrade cost for fiber optics and installation of the required switching and access equipment considering the existing lines quality.
- *Auditors' opinion*: external financial auditors' assessment of the investment from a pure accounting perspective.

Many decision factors were considered in the business plan justifying the $2.5 billion dollar investment in TWE. The purchase included the potential value of the synergy formed by the combined content, packaging and distribution of each alliance player. Content is provided solely by TWE. Packaging (how information is put together foreseeing all future services and capabilities) is provided by each alliance partners, and transport (how the information is transmitted) combines the capacity of all alliance partners. A large part of the investment represents access to TWE programming and content.

In choosing Time Warner as a partner, US West recognized that Time Warner saw technology as a means for achieving strategic goals. US West actively seeks partners that can boost productivity of its 70 000 employees through technology and will only ally with partners that see technology as being strategic.[6] Alliance projects are highly respected and assignment to alliance projects is viewed in a positive light. All those working on the Full Service Network alliance have a commitment to using technology for delivering entertainment and information to the home.

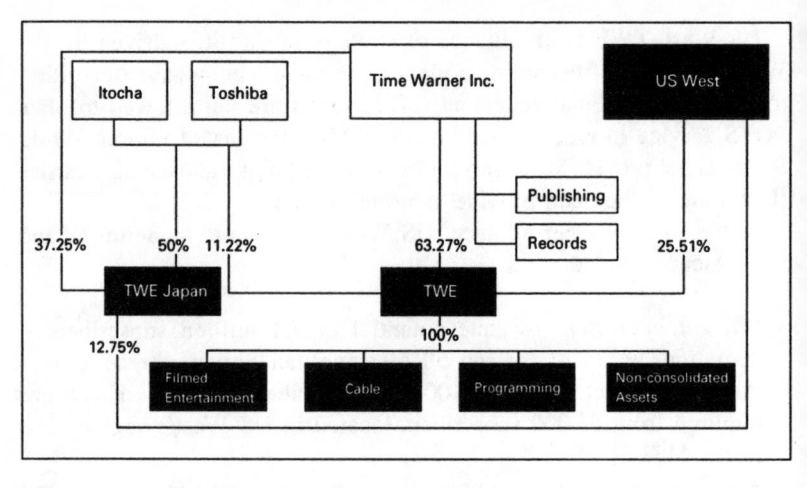

Source: 'Multimedia Services and Technology: Opportunities and Partnerships' (Englewood, CO: US West Multimedia Communications, Inc., October 26, 1993, 2).

Figure 3.3 Ownership Structure of Time Warner Entertainment

3.2 TIME WARNER'S PERSPECTIVE

Time Warner maintains majority control over its operations that include many alliances. As shown in Figure 3.3, Time Warner Inc. controls TWE with 63.27% of shares, US West, Itochu and Toshiba are all significant shareholders but do not hold any majority shares. Each partner recognizes potential of integrating Filmed Entertainment, Cable, Programming, and non-consolidated assets by bringing resources to the table. Time Warner is keeping partnership options open by not relinquishing control over any business units.

US West continues to acquire CATV properties out-of-region that can be upgraded to provide Full Service Network services. In July, 1994, US West acquired Wometco and Georgia Cable Television (GCTV) that exclusively serve the Atlanta area. After the $1.2 billion acquisition, US West began offering CATV programming to the Atlanta area through its Multimedia group. Tom Pardun, head of US West's Multimedia group, stated that US West fully intends to be a major provider of combined cable TV and telephony services in many parts of the country.[7] The alliance with Time Warner will be used to supply much of the programming for the Atlanta Systems.

Time Warner is investing in voice switches and has signed a deal worth several hundred million dollars with AT&T for 5ESS digital switches. The switches, commonly used for voice communications, will be installed for Time Warner in Rochester, NY and 25 other US cities. Time Warner targets cities for voice where the local exchange carrier (LEC) monopoly will soon be lifted and where an easy interconnection with existing Time Warner systems is possible. It also seeks to make as many 'friendly' interconnection agreements with local telephone carriers as possible. Time Warner targets both private and corporate markets, seeking an increasing amount of the Bells' voice business.

Some industry analysts believe it may be the content providers that assert control. The communications industries will provide the transport but the content is what actually differentiates one service from another. Time Warner is a key content provider with its ownership of (i) movie studios – Warner Brothers Studios; (ii) television stations – Cinemax, Home Box Office; (iii) music – Warner Music; (iv) magazines – *People*, *Fortune*, *Sports Illustrated*, *Southern Living* and *Vibe*. Time Warner's content holdings may provide lower cost and product differentiation that may be the key in marketing the US West–Time Warner partnership a leader in Information Superhighway businesses.

4 AT&T's Alliances

Isn't it sort of like putting Humpty Dumpty back together? (John L. Clendenin, chairman of BellSouth Corp., commenting on AT&T's McCaw takeover).

But the 'poor-little-me phenomenon' isn't relevant anymore. I can't be worried about antitrust matters when competition is fierce . . . Our challenge is to stay ahead (AT&T CEO Robert Allen, commenting on the anti-trust implications of the McCaw takeover).

4.1 ALLIANCE STRATEGY

The core of AT&T's alliance strategy is delivering the traffic generated from alliance partners and customers onto an AT&T-owned network. It is similar to General Electric's strategy in the 1920s when it manufactured small electrical appliances to increase demand for electricity and higher-priced power transmission equipment. AT&T generates demand for its network by increasing the number of devices that can use its network. Since AT&T owns the world's largest network with 80 million callers spending $40 billion annually, there is a good chance that new traffic will find its way onto an AT&Ts network. By forming strategic alliances with equipment providers (like appliance makers in the GE case), AT&T locks in traffic from that equipment maker. The idea is to turn the AT&T network into a hosting environment for alliance partners' equipment, software and services, and provide telecommunications services to end-users.

By allying with major applications developers, AT&T receives network billing receipts without administrative ownership of applications or information. AT&T provides only 'glueware' tying partners' applications together, enabling applications to integrate various services, such as America On-Line, CompuServe, and Prodigy.

AT&T expects the $900 billion global information market to reach $1.4 trillion by 1996. According to AT&T CEO, Robert Allen,

The global network is our core business. Many people literally live on the network with electronic mail and mailboxes to get their mes-

26

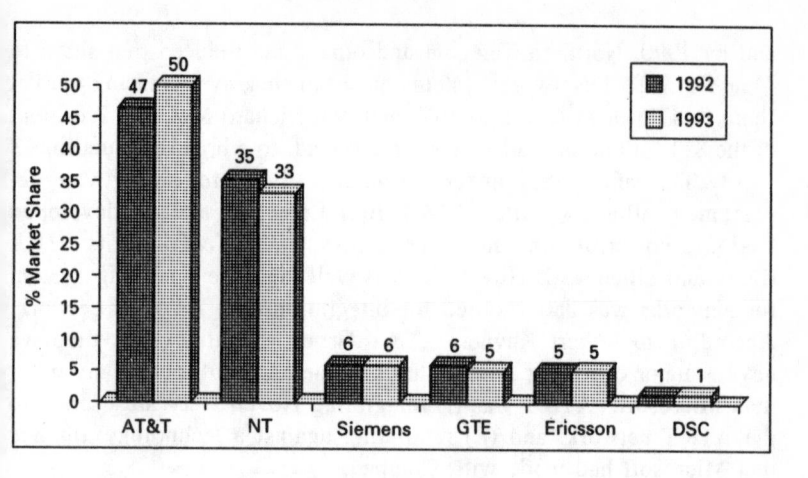

Source: Nortel Daily Information Service, September 1, 1993; available from Northern Business Information, Inc.

Figure 4.1   AT&T's Rising Share of the US Public Switch Market

sages. Our traffic will accelerate the double digit (growth) pace indefinitely.

CyberSpace, CyberWare, CyberTalk, etc. are modern terms describing Robert Allen's electronic world.

According to analyst Jack Grubman, 'AT&T is smack in the middle of every positive trend in high-tech worldwide.'[1] AT&T has alliances in cellular communication, computer software, electronic mail, personal digital assistants and HDTV. In April 1993, AT&T CEO Robert Allen explained that the company hopes to dominate the convergence of communications, computers and video technologies by cross-breeding new products from its various business units (22 in total). While AT&T has been known to have disparate fiefdoms in Long Distance, Equipment and Bell Labs, the recent introduction of 22 separate business units has forced cross-organisational cooperation.

AT&T Network Systems, the former Western Electric Company, generates 17% of AT&T's $65 billion in revenue and is broadening its sales strategy. The unit is actively developing two-way interactive cable TV-, high speed ATM-, and voice-switches. Network Systems is responsible for AT&T's multimedia evolution and customers have started moving their switching business back to AT&T (see Figure 4.1). In 1981, before the AT&T breakup, AT&T held 77% of the switch market

and by 1990, Northern Telecom and others had reduced that share to 41%. But AT&T Network Systems has been steadily increasing market share to 47% in 1992 and to 50% in 1993. Richard McGinn, President of the $11 billion unit, attributes the rebound 'to a broad product line'.[2]

AT&T's traffic policy in service alliances holds for its software development alliances. After AT&T Bell Labs had already developed UNIX, a powerful computer operating system, AT&T sold its UNIX rights and allied with Novell. The Novell Netware operating system for networks was better suited for integration onto AT&T's network. According to Robert Kavner, AT&T Group executive, 'it's time we have a major operating system that's in the hands of a company other than Microsoft.' AT&T was (i) integrating Novell NetWare users into the AT&T network, and (ii) retaliating against a technology alliance that Microsoft had made with Compaq.

Through alliances with both Novell Inc. and Lotus Development Corp., AT&T may soon have nationwide services for users of Lotus Notes and Novell Netware. AT&T will offer 'Public Data Services' as the platform for the AT&T Netware-based 'Network Notes' and the connect services. Rates for Public Data Services will run at $500 to $5000 per hour for dedicated access. The Data Services platform will allow optional access to AT&T's public data network and additional public messaging services.

In the area of personal digital assistants (PDAs), AT&T is almost entirely dependent on R&D through strategic alliances. The AT&T EasyLink Services unit is developing a messaging service based on the Telescript protocol. Telescript is a communications protocol developed at the General Magic alliance of which AT&T is a member. AT&T's PDAs will run on the Hobbit computer chip that was designed for external development from the beginning. According to William Warwick, president of AT&T Microelectronics, 'Our strategic plan called for eight partners [for Hobbit chip development] by the end of the year [1993] and we already have five.' AT&T's Hobbit partners include Matsushita, NEC, and Toshiba; they can develop Hobbit with four times more processing power per watt than Intel's 386DX processor. EasyLink's alliance with GO Corporation is developing the PenPoint mobile operating system specifically for its PDA. As a member, AT&T hopes the General Magic alliance will choose its wireless network for transport of traffic generated by PDA devices. In summary, all parts of the EasyLink business plan for entering the PDA market include strategic alliances.

The cellular business is a good example of AT&T using a partner to

enter a market and then acquiring that partner. AT&T sought a cellular alliance partner that would (a) increase brand identity and (b) avoid the local loop.[3] The value of AT&T's brand name combined with a service that could bypass the local Baby Bell monopolies was of great strategic value in the partnership.

What began as an alliance ended in one of the largest takeovers ever. AT&T had owned a 33% ($3.7 billion) stake in McCaw Cellular Communications while negotiating with McCaw and the Justice Department for acquisition approval. In late 1994, AT&T agreed to a purchase price of $12.6 billion and the Justice Department approved the deal.

AT&T would only rename the McCaw service, 'AT&T' after holding 100% equity in McCaw. According to Craig McCaw, 'AT&T is an incredible brand.' A customer survey showed that customers believed that AT&T was the best cellular phone company even before AT&T had provided a cellular service. McCaw renamed its service 'AT&T' as soon as possible after the acquisition.

The AT&T–McCaw alliance will change the local access market through McCaw's radio-based, cellular access to 35% of the US population. McCaw now has 2 million customers and can access 70 million more.[4] By bypassing the local Bell monopoly on residential access using wireless technology, interexchange carriers do not have to pay high access fees. The fees account for almost 50% of the charges for a local phone call and AT&T pays $20 billion annually in such fees. Long-distance service providers dread 'the last mile' and will do anything to minimize its cost.

For access to the $128 billion Western European telecommunications market,[5] AT&T has chosen to team with Unisource, a consortium of the Swedish, Dutch and Swiss PTTs, SITA, Telefonica, Singapore Telecom and KDD Telecom (Japan). Unisource will buy into AT&T's World Partners programme and use the AT&T technical platform.

Some of AT&T's major strategic partners are outlined in Table 4.1. It appears that AT&T is using robust alliance tactics in line with its classic history of corporate strategy.

4.2 BELL LABORATORIES

AT&T Bell Laboratories is studying materials engineering, communications logistics, and other key technologies needed to make the

Table 4.1   AT&T's Major Alliances

AT&T Partner	Agreement Type	Techn/Bus. Area	Product	Date
Apple, IBM Siemens	VERSIT Consort.	Comp/Tel Integ.	PDAs	11/94
BroadBand Techs	Joint Development	Fiber-Coax. Mixing	CATV sys.	10/6/94
Compaq Computer	Techn.-sharing	Computers	Pen–mobile	4/93
Eo Corp.	Alliance	Persona Comm. mkt	Hand-held Cp.	NA
General Magic	Consortium	PDAs, Telescript	EasyLink	
General Instment	Consortium	Multimedia	NA	NA
Go Corp.	Alliance	Wireless	Pen–wireless	NA
Hoya	Alliance	Japan mkt	Photomasks	NA
Hewlett-Packard	Alliance	Multimedia dialtone	Worldworx	6/1994
IBM	Alliance	IBM-Intelligent	Agent-based	
IBM		Communic. services	comm.	8/12/94
ImagiNation	R&D funding	Interactive,	ImagiNation	7/93
ImagiNation		On-line games	Network	
Intel Corp	Co-marketing	Interactive Video	PC-Vid conf.	1/94
Intel	Alliance	PC nets, ICs	UNIX, LANs	NA
Italcable	Joint marketing	European	Net Eqpt	NA
Italtel	Alliance	Europe services	Telecomm.	NA
Lotus Devel.	Alliance	Public Notes servers	Net. notes	1994
Lucky-Gold-Star	Alliance	Asian services	Fiber, ICs	NA
Mannesman	Alliance	German OEM	M-wave radio	NA
Matsush., NEC, Tosh.	Alliance	Microprocessors	Hobbit	NA
McCaw Cellular	Acquisition	Cellular Service	Service-only	10/94
Microsoft	Informal Coop.	Interoperability	Software	1994
Mitsubishi	Alliance	Semicon. techn.	SRAM, GaS	NA
NA Wireless, C&W	Alliance	Wireless	PCS	11/94
NEC	Alliance	Japan services	IC, CAD, cell	NA
NCR	Acquisition	Computer Systems	CPE Equip	NA
Nokia Cell. Phones	Marketing	Cellular Phones	OEM	4/21/94
Novell Corp.	Alliance	TSAPI	NetWare	5/94
NV Philips	Alliance	Europe services	PCBs	acq. 90
Olivetti	Alliance	Europe OEM	Office Equip.	NA
PacBell, NASA,				
GTE, Rockwell,	Joint trial	SMDS	NA	NA
Silicon Graphics, Inc.	Alliance	Cable TV switches	Orlando	6/22/94
Stratacom	Alliance	Telecommunication	ATM-FR	1/93
Sony Corp.	Marketing alliance	Communicators	Magic link	9/28/94
Telefonica	Alliance	Europe mkt	Net Eqpt	NA
Time Warner	Joint trial	Multimedia, CATV	ATM, video	3/1994
Unisource	World partners	Voice and data	Services	6/23/94
Unitel	Consortium	Voice and data	ISDN V-Route	11/92
Viac., PacTel, GTE	Joint test	CATV	Video, ATM	8/94
Xerox Corp.	Alliance	Remote printing	Publish, SW	1994
XIWT Group	Alliance	GII	NII stds	NA
Zenith	Alliance	Digital compress.	HDTV	NA

Note: NA Not available.

Information Superhighway a reality. AT&T Bell Laboratories receives over $3 billion in funding every year and has averaged a patent a day for almost 70 years.[6] AT&T employs 18 000 software designers versus only 2000 at software giant, Microsoft. According to Nathan Myhrvold, vice president of Microsoft's Advanced Technology and

Business Development, 'AT&T always had Chinese armies of software developers.' Many industry observers feel that a single entity like Bell Labs can act more swiftly and competitively than a consortium like Bellcore.

Before divestiture, Bell Labs had surrounded itself with an aura that its stores of knowledge would blow everyone away when free to compete. But according to Michael Noll, a former AT&T marketing executive:

> One reason AT&T agreed to divestiture was to be free to develop the many new business opportunities that supposedly were available from the technological storehouse of Bell Labs. This hypothesis was not investigated before divestiture. After divestiture AT&T Bell Labs did an internal study of all its ideas for new products, services and businesses. While at AT&T I had the opportunity to review the results of this study, a multi-volumed document. Of the hundreds of ideas submitted, fewer than half a dozen, as I recall, were realistic, and most of them were already under development in some fashion. The simple fact was that the Labs' cupboard was bare. the jewels of the Bell System, the operating telephone companies, had been given away for nothing.[7]

Although AT&T doubled its lab staffing from 1984 to 1987, it was not able to capitalize on free market opportunities. After 1987, AT&T increasingly used strategic alliances to develop new products and markets. The internal markets created by AT&T's 20 business units for Bell Labs' products were not sufficient to drive R&D into full competitiveness. Despite the huge and almost unmatched R&D capabilities at Bell Labs, many market opportunities continue to be filled through alliance partners.

5 Multimedia Alliances

Our goal [in alliance-making] is to use technological breakthroughs and new entertainment delivery systems to provide consumers with a compelling and creative array of programming ... The essence of entertainment will not change. What has always counted is the story and the skill with which it is told, and that is what Disney is all about (Michael Eisner, CEO of Walt Disney, commenting on the alliance with BellSouth, Southwestern Bell and Ameritech).[1]

There's no way a small CD [-ROM multimedia] company can get to market right now without a big partner ... Having a big partner also greases the skids for raising more money' to keep the company growing (Julie Schwerin, president of InfoTech, a Woodstock, VT, firm that tracks the multimedia industry).[2]

Our strategy was to identify the most compelling interest categories measured by consumer spending and then go find the best partner from a brand and content perspective ... Our partners are doing it because they don't want to be left behind in new media and they have zero risk doing it with us (Len Jordan, head of marketing for Creative Multimedia).[3]

Multimedia generally refers to integrated voice, data and video services on the Information Superhighway. Multimedia products integrate voice, data and video into one device that provides visual and audio sensations. Each of these sensations can be interactive to make the users feel like being a part of the story or information.

By providing users with multimedia services, significant improvements in the computer are possible. For example, CD-ROM-based computers have video applications which allow a user to browse movies, encyclopedias, wildlife specials and so on. Teachers and professors can create highly-customized curricula by piecing together an entire course from on-line reading materials. Students can study the curriculum using actual video and audio clips that complement the reading sources. Students can study history by playing different scenarios to find out what history predicts the outcome in each case would be.

News services such as Reuter's that are incorporated in multimedia systems are automatically updated as news and information becomes available. Keeping abreast of new developments makes learning more relevant and allows students to 'hit the real world' running. The transition to the 'real world' can be accelerated by multimedia interviewing, coaching, and videoconferencing.

Alliances between large and small companies are becoming popular in multimedia. Small companies have the entrepreneurial drive and artistic talents to develop high quality CD-ROMs. The small company first allies with a content partner (for example, museum, artist, etc.) and transfers information into an integrated program on CD-ROM. For example, Creative Multimedia develops CD-ROM titles from partners such as Time Warner, Inc., Fodor's Travel Publications and the Smithsonian Institution.[4]

The CD-ROM developer then forms an alliance with a service provider that can provide public access to the CD-ROM through the Information Superhighway. Small companies ally with the owners of networks such as telephone and cable companies that add new programming to their networks. CD-ROM makers receive a royalty for each customer that accesses their service and they, in turn, pay a royalty to the original content providers. For example, Creative Multimedia pays a partner $20 000–50 000 in royalties for a title that may have cost $300 000 to develop. Its overall revenue will depend on how many persons buy or access its CD-ROM service.

Service providers take virtually no risk in these alliances since they are a contractual arrangement that acquires CD-ROMs and provides payment to owners on an as-used basis. As new CD-ROMs become available, the telephone company can decide how best to add to a programming portfolio. It is a win-win situation and a natural for increasing content, an area regarded as strategically vital to service providers. Customers benefit by having the most popular and up to date selection of multimedia services.

Interconnecting multimedia devices can be more specifically labeled as the National Information Infrastructure. The Clinton administration's National Information Infrastructure Initiative will interlink research facilities, government offices, businesses, universities and theaters. It will allow for a free exchange of information that creates synergies within and between industries that have never cooperated before.

The increased communication should lead to another industrial revolution in terms of 'iterative speed up'. The feedback loops and interactions between far-flung colleagues should greatly accelerate and

promote advancements in the sciences, arts, humanities and business. By providing video as well as voice communication, the Information Superhighway offers a more powerful and more pleasurable way of doing business long-distance.

Instead of eliminating travel, the use of multimedia for video-conferencing has increased the effectiveness of distance communications and emphasized the importance of regular, personal meetings. Videoconferencing has shown that regular personal meetings are more important than ever. Productivity at in-person meetings is increased through homework done in videoconferencing sessions.

Strategic alliances provide the perfect means for developing common goals between related but disparate businesses. Strategic alliances between companies require an enormous amount of inter-corporate communication to build trust and pursue common goals. Often the related companies cannot afford new communication systems just so their companies can be compatible. Existing communication systems must often suffice and face-to-face, telephone, and fax communication are primarily used.

The National Information Infrastructure allows separate businesses to communicate by complying with standards set by Bellcore. Every company in the world will soon have some means for full multimedia communication. Common standards and a multimedia infrastructure will promote better communication. The efficient creation of highly focused alliances requires short start up times critical for capitalizing on brief windows of opportunity. That should promote better partner matches, more capitalized market opportunities, and shorter product life-cycles.

Creating multimedia technology requires partners to jointly research, develop, manufacture, and distribute new products. As shown in Figure 5.1, companies from all realms of information, entertainment and communications are part of the pie. Through the efforts of these alliances, disparate industries are creating products that provide several competitive advantages in one product. For example, a recent alliance combines the set-top cable TV technology of Scientific Atlanta, the communications technology of Siemens Stromberg-Carlson and the computer technology of Sun Microsystems. The results of this alliance will be a set-top multimedia computer, not just a 'channel clicker'.

Joint testing of new products is conducted by the alliance partners in determining the scale of a technology push. If a product needs to be further developed, joint development proceeds until the market pulls the technology out. Once the product is introduced, each partner may increase component content in an attempt to control the direction of

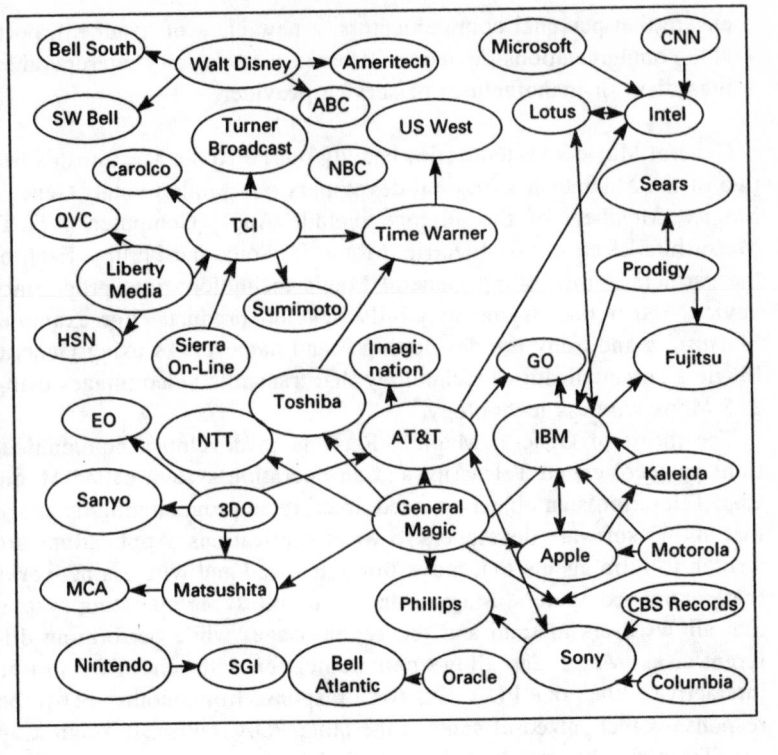

Source: Wetzel, J.M., 'Multimedia: Facts, Fiction, and Opportunities' (Englewood, CO: US West Multimedia Communications, Inc., 1994, 1).

Figure 5.1 Multimedia Alliances

development. After achieving the product introduction goals, alliances must reassess the future of a business relationship.

Some of the major multimedia alliances are described below. Particular emphasis has been placed on those companies that are developing PC-based systems. For information on cable TV–telephone ventures please refer to Chapters 2 and 3.

General Magic will be one of the major alliances that fuels the devices and road-signs on the Information Superhighway. General Magic was spun off from an internal venture at Apple Computer in 1990 to develop personal digital assistants. Its goal is to develop technology and standards combining fax, electronic mail, paging, and communication via modem, or cellular telephony over regular telephone lines.[5] General Magic's mission is to

ensure that personal communicators, a new class of handheld, portable communications devices will be easy to use and interoperable, regardless of manufacturer or service provider.[6]

General Magic's system relies heavily on the Apple Macintosh since two of the Macintosh's original developers left Apple to start General Magic.[7] Members of the alliance include Apple Computer, AT&T, Matsushita Electric, Oki Electric, Motorola, Sony and Philips. Each of the partners is integrating General Magic technology into proprietary devices rather than trying to jointly develop products. For example, Matsushita and Sony are developing brand-name PDAs using General Magic's communications technology that transmits video images using 2–5 Mbps wireless technology.[8]

The thrust of General Magic's R&D is to develop a communications protocol called Telescript and an operating system called Magic Cap. Telescript is an object-oriented, interpreted programming language that allows software developers to write applications. Applications are written to form agents that move through wired and wireless networks that connect computers. Magic Cap is a multitasking operating system that allows users to send and receive messages while performing different tasks. Magic Cap allows communication with other PDAs to be interactive. When one PDA asks for a response from another PDA, the response is recognized as soon as the other PDA replies. If Magic Cap and Telescript become the *de facto* industry standard, users will be able to access all PDAs and networks connected with the National Information Infrastructure.

Since they are great manufacturers of consumer electronics, Japanese companies are keen to gain the insight necessary for Information Superhighway-compatible devices. For example, Matsushita, Oki and Sony are members of the General Magic consortium and Sumitomo has purchased a minority stake in Telecommunications International (TCI).[9] Japanese investments often rely on development partnerships to absorb and imitate technologies that are then mass-produced in Japan. The Japanese are notoriously good manufacturers and American partners seek their expertise in manufacturing technology. The Japanese are also interested in American 'content' that can be communicated via multimedia devices. For example, Matsushita–MCA, Sony–Columbia–CBS Records, Itochu-Toshiba–Time Warner are key alliances in entertainment. The result should be an increase in Japanese technologies in Information Superhighway products.

The many devices that access to the Information Superhighway will

include not only PDAs but also computers and televisions. IBM has announced a hardware alliance with Motorola and a software alliance with Apple to develop a next-generation multimedia computer. The alliance will set its own desktop standards in multimedia personal computing. The new multimedia computer is powered by the IBM/Motorola PowerPC chip that competes with Intel's Pentium chip. Apple Computer is also introducing PowerPC-based Macintosh computers. Since Microsoft and Intel will control 85% of the desktop PC market,[10] PowerPC is first targeting higher-end business users before entering the mass consumer market.[11] The combined power of IBM, Motorola and Apple should provide enough technological leverage to engender new multimedia standards in personal computing.

Video games now represent a $6.5 million a year business[12] and are a profitable part of the multimedia picture. Previously, Nintendo and Sega controlled the video game market but now AT&T, Matsushita, Paramount, Viacom, Blockbuster, IBM, Silicon Graphics, and Time Warner are entering the market. The video game market is extremely challenging to enter and its profitability drives players to form alliances to break Nintendo and Sega's hold.

For example, the start-up company, 3DO, has developed a CD-ROM player that allows users to interact with video. One of 3DO's strategic alliance partners, Electronic Arts, has developed video games that can be played on the 3DO device. The user plays the video game and interacts with imaginary racers and race events. For example, the motorcycle game, *Road Rash* has parties, bulletin boards, stores, and earnings that accompany the car and motorcycle races. Between races, players can choose to fraternize with other racers, purchase a new motorcycle or simply race again. The characters are comical and the effects are surprisingly realistic. As graphics quality improves, the 3DO system may appeal to a wider audience as a source of camaraderie and entertainment.

Hollywood film studios have become key multimedia content providers and the most popular alliance partners for programming content. Several Bells including Ameritech and SNET have hired former Hollywood executives to negotiate strategic alliances with film studios. Film studios search for computer and telecommunications partners that can generate an additional $10 million[13] in annual sales. Alliances provide national exposure for movies, television, talent shows, video games, and home video products. The joint synergy of studio-Bells makes the following possible: movies on demand, home shopping, interactive games, educational programs and travel assistance. The alliances are win-win

– studios receive extra distribution and the Bells develop competitive programming.

The Bells hope to attract Walt Disney, Paramount, Viacom and Time Warner films into combined telephone–entertainment packages. Examples of studio–Bell alliances include Time Warner–US West, Viacom–NYNEX, and Walt Disney–BellSouth, Southwestern Bell, and Ameritech.

One of America's most famous studios, Walt Disney, has long been reluctant to enter into the alliance game. The competitive nature of entertainment has changed so much that Disney has been forced to take a more active alliance tack. With pressure from other Disney executives and prodding from neighboring Bells: BellSouth, Southwest Bell, and Ameritech, Disney is forming alliances. Disney's partners now access films from Walt Disney Pictures, Miramax Films, Touchstone Pictures, and Hollywood Pictures.

The Bells programming packages are designed to compete against existing cable television offerings. Since there used to be little competition in programming, households were wired for only one cable television provider. Using multimedia technology, telephone service providers offer a second main source of competition. Viewers can choose from either the cable or telephone company depending on price and quality.

The set-top box common to most cable television systems will become a full-blown multimedia computer. Oracle is developing a video database that will allow service providers to store programming locally. The device is called the Media Server and viewers can request movies and multimedia services from the Media Server. Oracle has started its certification programme to ensure compatibility between set-top boxes and multimedia database software. It hopes to create a dominant design for multimedia database technology that encourages independent software developers. Several companies are developing multimedia software and point of sale technology that will be integrated into the next generation set-top boxes.

Not all alliances result in practise developments for the partners. The alliance between Oracle and Lotus is an example of rivalry between internal groups and strategic alliances in the multimedia market. Lotus has the most competitive workgroup software available called Lotus Notes with 900 000 users in 3500 companies.[14] Workgroup software allows geographically dispersed work groups to cooperate as if they were together. Oracle decided to pursue the workgroup market through its Document software and ConText search engine. Although spokepersons refer to Document and Notes as being complementary, engineers at Oracle call Document the 'Notes Killer'.[15] In fact, Notes

already uses the Oracle database and Document's introduction has made Lotus a takeover target. Internal groups at the two companies competed so hard to keep the products separate and preserve separate corporate identities that IBM was able to intervene and buy Lotus.

Lotus Development Corp. and Intel Corp. have formed a joint development and marketing agreement for video-conferencing and computer data products.[16] Under the agreement, Lotus will base its Lotus Notes products on Intel's ProShare personal conferencing technology. The Intel ProShare system adds video and audio functionality to Lotus Notes for true multimedia workgroup technology. The workgroup functionality of Intel's ProShare competes against AT&T's Telemedia Personal Video System.

In summary, the major multimedia players are creating a multimedia pie. Strategic alliances between the information, entertainment and communication industries allow the multimedia pie to bake. Once these technologies develop fully, there may be jockeying to divide up the pie. It is likely that alliance partners (as shown in Figure 5.1) may acquire players that are eating more than their share. Eventually multimedia services may serve as a model of how industries are created and matured solely through strategic alliances.

6 The German Market

This is a market you have to be involved with. It's too big to stay away. The rush is on to see who will get a joint venture going first and then hope that the German government will give them a license to set up a telephone system (Hans Peter Peters, Managing Director, Morgan Stanley, Frankfurt, Germany).

Germany is an attractive market for international carriers because of its huge business community and the archaic tariffs companies are now being offered. The country will go from being one of Europe's most closed markets to one of its most competitive (Eva Miller, London-based analyst for Lehman Brothers Ltd.).[1]

6.1 INTRODUCTION

The German market is a critical link in the international expansion of major telecommunications companies. The German national phone company, the Deutsche Bundespost Telekom (DBP), is the third largest telecommunications company in the world after NTT and AT&T. DBP now holds a monopoly on all German consumer voice and data services valued at $40 billion and expected to grow to $70 billion by 2003. The German telecommunications market is expected to reach $100 billion by the year 2000.[2] A small number of German cellular and private network resellers exist but they are no match for DBP's monopoly. A long painful period of deregulation will be experienced before competitors break into much of DBP's revenue.

DBP is enormous and has many characteristics of a monopoly power. It has 230 000 employees servicing 37 million phone lines resulting in 62.6 employees per 10 000 phone lines (see Figure 6.1).[3] That ratio is far higher than any of the impending foreign players that are making partnerships on DBP's turf. DBP itself is worth DM70–DM100 billion ($45–$64 billion) and its profits run at $30 per line. German courts have increasingly scrutinized possible cross-subsidization of DBP's DATEX-P network from other DBP service revenues.

In 1992, the US had a $3.3 billion trade deficit in telecommunications[4] with a $250 million imbalance in settlements between the DBP

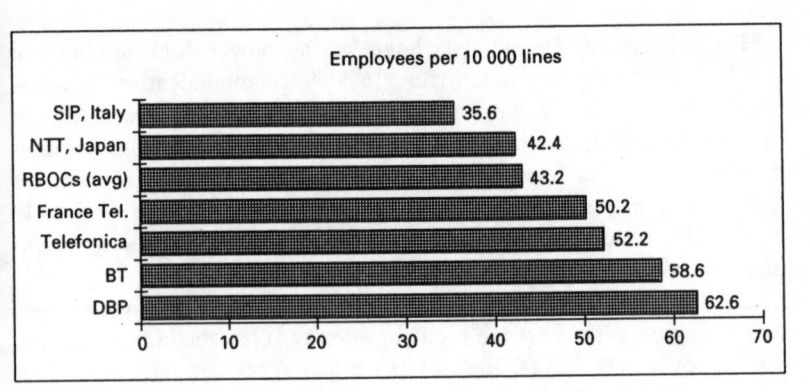

Employees per 10 000 lines

SIP, Italy	35.6
NTT, Japan	42.4
RBOCs (avg)	43.2
France Tel.	50.2
Telefonica	52.2
BT	58.6
DBP	62.6

Source: 1993 Company Reports (OECD).

Figure 6.1   Comparison of Employees per 10 000 Phone Lines

and US carriers in 1992.[5] US operators feel the accounting rate system is discriminatory. The accounting rate system uses a fixed percentage of Special Drawing Rights (SDRs) owed to a foreign carrier. For example, when DBP receives a call from the US, it charges a certain percentage to complete the call. Similarly, for a call from Germany to the US, US carriers charge a percentage to complete the call. The difference is that German calling tariffs are considerably higher so Germany is paid a higher percentage of the total revenues received from calls in both directions. This is the essence of the settlements imbalance.

To help eliminate the imbalance, DBP cut its accounting rate by 43%. US operators want to eliminate any rate-based inequities by negotiating partnerships on a cost-accounting basis. Cost accounting is a wholesale type arrangement that charges based on the cost of the call. It promotes more equitable revenue sharing for international calling with different tariff systems.

Although Germany is the third largest telecommunications market behind the US and Japan, it is truly underdeveloped in terms of technology, Most consumers rely on outdated rotary pulse dialing without enhanced services such as call waiting, voice messaging, and dial-back. DBP offers no new number notification, call forwarding or call redirection. Lack of itemized billing makes it difficult for customers to inspect or dispute billing. Waiting times for new telephones or new lines are commonly six to eight weeks. Directory service and directory assistance are often unreachable during the busy hours.

The German market with its huge buying power, high pricing and low service levels is a dream for global telecommunications players. The sheer size and vulnerability of the German market to local and foreign players makes it *the* strategic market for 1996. Telecommunications players such as AT&T, Sprint, BT and France Telecom are committing major funding towards developing the German market. In fact, DBP is truly worried that efforts of both local and foreign competitors will crumble the monopoly.

DBP is reevaluating its competitive stance on a more international basis. Its operating costs are high considering it has the highest number of employees per 10 000 lines of any major service provider (see Figure 6.1). Half of DBP's employees are civil servants who are untouchable in case of layoffs. Non-civil servant administration may be affected by a 10–15% total reduction in workforce from 230 000 to 200 000.

On January 1, 1998, DBP's monopoly status will be lifted and privatization will begin. The German government plans an initial sale of $10 billion in DBP stock with more rounds following. The investment banking firm, Goldman Sachs, was chosen with the consultation of Bundeskanzler Helmut Kohl for administering the lucrative stock sale.

The German Postal Ministry is allowing DBP to control all infrastructure ownership until well after the stock sale. Technically, even after liberalization, DBP will own all infrastructure, wires, lines and switches. Foes to the monopoly on infrastructure are seeking partners positioned with strategic assets. Liberalization forces fear discrimination in access to requisite lines and equipment. A major issue is how much competitors must pay for DBP's lines in competing against DBP.[6] Clearly, the German Postal Ministry wants to preserve value for the stock sale.

6.2   STRATEGIC ALLIANCES

Germany has become a testing ground for alliances changing a foreign market. It can be said that every rising player has made or is making a strategic alliance in Germany. Investment in German alliances and joint ventures should reach $12 billion by 1997. An overview of German alliances is outlined in Figure 6.2.

Foreign carriers such as Sprint, BT, and AT&T, either have formed or are trying to form alliances. The US Justice Department and the European Commission are scrutinizing alliances and Sprint has not yet been allowed to ally with DBP and France Telecom. But the EU is

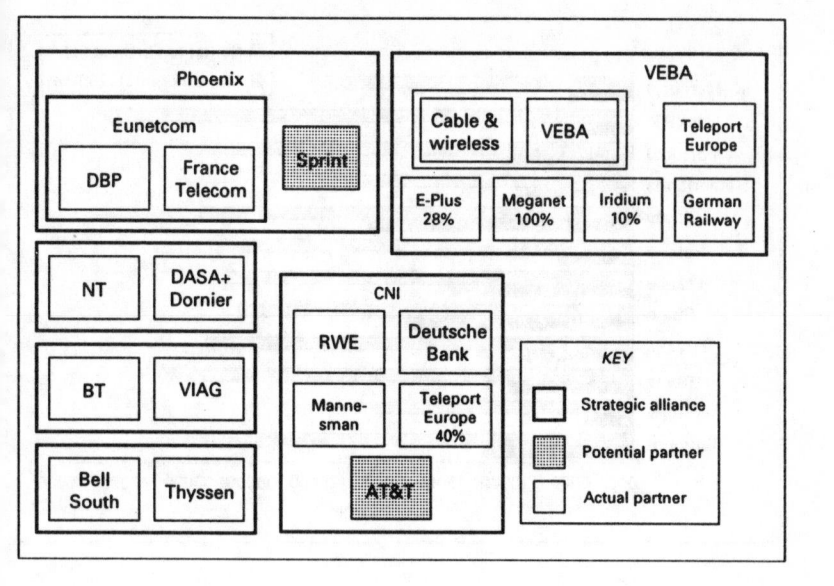

Figure 6.2   Alliances in Germany

careful not to restrict competition too much since all EU countries must deregulate by 1998.

6.2.1 DBP's Alliances

Alliances play contrary to the strategy of DBP which continues to be a 'go it alone' player. In fact, DBP has the least number of alliances of any operator in Europe with only two compared to France Telecom's seventeen. Evidence of DBP's few alliances can be found in its high prices for trans-European leased lines. Figure 6.3 shows the monthly rental rates for 2Mbps leased lines for both national, 250 kilometer, and international circuits. Even though Germany is situated centrally in Europe, its monthly rates to furthest EC states are the third highest in Europe. This suggests that DBP has few tariff-reducing arrangements with European countries for reducing the costs of circuits crossing multiple countries. A common goal of European alliances is to reduce line costs crossing multiple countries and reduce end-to-end service prices.

On December 7, 1993, DBP allied with France Telecom in the Phoenix alliance. Phoenix plans to buy 20% of Sprint for $4.2 billion and combine the revenues of Sprint, France Telecom and DBP totalling revenues of $70 billion. Pending EU Commission and US Justice Department

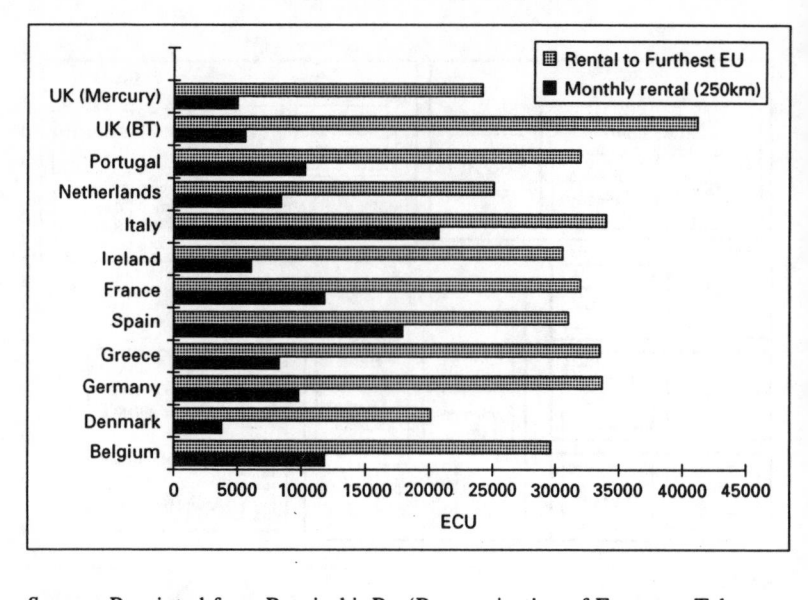

Source: Reprinted from Pospischi, R., 'Reorganization of European Telecoms: The Cases of British Telecom, France Telecom, and Deutsche Telecom' (*Telecommunications Policy*, 17, November 1993, 612. © Butterworth Heinemann, Oxford.

Figure 6.3   Prices of European 2Mbps Leased Line Circuits

approval, Phoenix would become one of the largest telecommunications players in the world.

Phoenix wants Sprint to become a major player in the North American marketplace. Because of misgivings about reciprocity in market access, the US Justice Department is holding up approval for the Sprint deal. In fact AT&T tried to ally with Eunetcom but had no luck in persuading the Justice Department. It does not appear that the Justice Department will budge on German–American partnerships until the German market is opened up.

Although it can be said that this alliance is even larger than AT&T (1994 revenues of $67 billion) it is doubtful that these three companies will really put their entire operations into the alliance. The net result is an alliance that actually has its own revenue only equal to the amount that partner companies commit. Most operations except those specifically designated for the alliance will be kept separate in the foreseeable future.

Both DBP and France Telecom are remaining cautious about com-

mitting personnel to Eunetcom, an outsourcing unit of Phoenix. Eunetcom is hiring new people rather than allowing DBP and France Telecom to shift employees into the alliance. Eunetcom is starting with a free-spirited, enjoyable, motivated corporate culture, eschewing the civil servant mentality. In fact, the Eunetcom director of operations is only 33 years old, unheard of in a seniority-based promotional system. The combination of a free-spirited mentality and the funding of its parent companies could make Eunetcom a very competitive telecommunications company.

Eunetcom is actively pursuing customers and entry into the North American market. Its first customer was worth $200 million over five years[7] and was acquired by purchasing the networking services of Dun & Bradstreet's DunsNet. DunsNet provides data communications services for the Dun & Bradstreet companies, a role that Eunetcom now assumes. Its second customer was IBM for managed transmission services in 40 locations in six European countries. Its third customer was Group Bull for managed services of the corporate backbone network.

Operations facilities are kept separate from the parents with each partner holding one-third ownership. Communications hubs based on time-division multiplexing (TDM) are located in Germany, France, the UK, the Netherlands, Belgium, Spain, Italy, and the US. Sprint, DBP and France Telecom will jointly invest in a global asynchronous transmission mode (ATM) network to replace the TDM hubs. Sprint will own 50% of the network and DBP and France Telecom, 25% each.

6.2.2 Foreign-Partner Alliances

Railways and electric utility companies such as Veba, RWE AG, and Viag AG have become popular strategic alliance partners because they own sophisticated electrical distribution grids. Electric utilities and railways have electrical distribution grids under the rail lines capable of housing fiber optics. Alliances provide funding for laying fiber optics and installing switching equipment. There is nothing illegal about setting up the equipment as long as it is not used to provide consumer voice services. As soon as liberalization allows, services can be provided using the newly-laid fiber optics.

The Communications Network International GmbH (CNI) alliance is targeting the corporate markets. The main founder, RWE AG, is an electrical utility operating primarily in the German industrial Rhine and Ruhr valleys. The second partner, Deutsche Bank, has been an important force against DBP's continued monopoly and lobbied in Bonn

to eliminate the monopoly. CNI won the fourth national cellular license in a nationwide bid. AT&T is expected to announce its partnership in CNI that will give it access to the German market.[8] Other partners include Mannesman Mobilfunk, the second largest German cellular operator and Teleport Europe, the European operation of the five-member US cable consortium. CNI is well positioned with a full range of corporate data, cellular and voice capabilities.

BellSouth's expansion efforts to capture DBP's core business included an alliance with Thyssen AG. Thyssen is Germany's seventh largest company with annual sales of $22 billion in steel, trading and services. The partnership with BellSouth signals a corporate commitment to its cellular, satellite and corporate networking capabilities. BellSouth and Thyssen own a combined stake of 49% in the mobile operator, E-Plus Mobilfunk. It is interesting that competing consortia, VEBA–C&W and Thyssen–BellSouth own a combined 77% stake in E-Plus. Eventually, one of the owners might buy out control of E-Plus and form one of the world's largest cellular networks.

Veba has partnered with Cable & Wireless plc (C&W) to develop telecom interests in countries outside the UK. Veba is a large German company with 128 000 employees and over $43 billion in annual sales.[9] Veba will spend $4 billion over the next ten years on its communications conglomerate.[10] Cable & Wireless is one of the world's largest voice and data operators and plans to invest $3.1 billion to develop European strategic partnerships. C&W welcomed Veba as a partner and both companies will combine assets as much as possible. Veba will purchase 10.5% of C&W shares and gain one non-executive seat on C&W's board. A 50:50 joint venture will be formed to pursue telecommunications services in European countries except for Germany, the UK, and Switzerland.

The German market for corporate fiber optics transmission services will be pursued through a joint venture called Vebacom GmbH. Vebacom will be 55%-owned by Veba and 45%-owned by C&W with Veba having management control. Veba's electric utility infrastructure and fiber optics may eventually be used for carrying consumer voice and data services. Veba has been laying fiber optic cable along the power lines of its Preussen Elektra subsidiary.[11]

Veba also owns 28% of E-Plus Mobilfunk, the third largest German cellular operator after DBP and Mannesman. Additional assets of Veba that will be folded into Vebacom include 10% of Motorola's Iridium satellite consortium and a 75% stake in Meganet for X.25 data communications. By combining partners' strategic assets, Vebacom is ideally

positioned to become a licensed German telecommunications operator after liberalization in 1998.

British Telecommunications plc has made a joint venture with Viag AG to provide voice and data communication for corporate networks. Viag is one of Germany's ten largest companies with annual sales totaling over $64 billion. Its core businesses are in energy, packaging, chemicals, and logistics, although its corporate networking subsidiary has some telecommunications experience. The Viag/BT alliance is called Viag InterKom and will provide services now offered by the BT/MCI venture as well as German services. Both Viag and BT will invest $980 million into expanding Viag's fiber optic base in Germany. According to Mina Jacqueline, head of Viag's telecom alliance, total investment depends on whether Viag would be able to provide services over its 4000 kilometers of fiber optic cable owned by its Bayerwerk subsidiary.[12] InterKom will start with 350 employees and will increase to 1000 in the short term. After Viag receives a license to be a full service provider, it hopes for annual sales of $622.6 million (DM 1 billion) by 1998.

The German market is interesting to watch as a playground of alliances. Partnerships are formed in the face of a monopoly, heavy regulatory control and large technology investments. Alliances, only recently becoming popular, are now common as companies position themselves before competition really begins.

7 Wireless Communications

Everybody can't possibly survive . . . With all these players – cellular, PCS, satellites – wireless is quickly becoming a commodity. It's going to be chaotic and bloody (Barry Goodstadt, Director of wireless industry consulting for Electronic Data Systems Corp.).[1]

The regional Bell companies are worried about access business because they are slowly but surely seeing their market erode (FCC Commissioner, Andrew Barrett).[2]

7.1 INTRODUCTION

Wireless communications has taken many established players by surprise and few recognized the huge growth of wireless technology. Players with experience providing radios to the military were the initial winners in cellular manufacturing. General Electric, Motorola, France's Matra Hachette, Sweden's L.M. Ericsson and Finland's Nokia recognized the value of the cellular market early – on and are now reaping tremendous profits from that foresight. Other manufacturers are using strategic alliances as a means of catching-up in cellular markets. A key goal of an alliance is to integrate one partner's wireless technology with the other partner's line-based switching equipment.

In the 1960s, Nokia was building field radios for Finnish soldiers and making equipment for the state-run phone company. In the late 1970s, Nokia was present when the telecom authorities of Sweden, Denmark, Norway, and Finland made plans to build the world's first international cellular network. In 1988, Nokia sold off its no-growth businesses (toilet paper, boots, and power cables) to concentrate on telecommunications. In 1990, Nokia was still losing money and struggling with an identity crisis. Mobile phones only accounted for 8% of total net sales of $5.6 billion.[3] In responding to the growing opportunity in cellular, Nokia bet almost the entire company on cellular as its core concern. Sari Baldauf who heads Nokia's cellular systems division, says,

Some of the big telecommunications companies thought wireless was a pretty small market niche. But we saw it as an opportunity.[4]

Early on Nokia recognized cellular's potential, and pumped huge amounts of R&D into its wireless technology showing good timing in a technological window. After reaching a certain saturation point, markets lose their strategic significance as new suppliers enter and competition heats up. In attempting to make up for lost product development time, many established telecommunications players scramble for partners and hope to capture even a fraction of the opportunity missed. The cellular powerhouse, Nokia, changed its entire core business by betting the company's future on the right technology at the right time.

North America is now the largest market for cellular, 16 million subscribers at the end of 1993,[5] 14 000 new subscribers each day, and a 25% annual growth rate. But other countries lead in terms of cellular POTS growth ratios. For example, in Eastern Europe, 'leapfrog (cellular) technologies' are seen as the sole means of bypassing outdated terrestrial land-line systems. The cost of installing terrestrial lines is prohibitive and not feasible in comparison to cellular.

Many countries, both developing and developed, have recognized the potential of cellular. Among them:

- *Mexico*: Cellular phone use is increasing at about 82% annually, twice as fast as in the United States.[6]
- *Sri Lanka*: Five years ago the government decided cellular was the quickest way to provide the population with phones. In promoting cellular, it reduced import duties from 40% to zero.[7] Today, Sri Lankans recognize cellular as the fastest and easiest way to get a telephone. Prices have dropped from $2500 in 1989 to $250 in 1994.
- *Singapore*: The mobile phone sector has grown at a compounded rate of 76% in the last five years.[8] In 1997, Singapore Telecom loses its monopoly status and Motorola, BellSouth, Mobile Data, Vodafone, Cable & Wireless, and HongKong Telecom will seek cellular licenses.
- *UK*: Cellular subscription now outpaces POTS subscription. The UK's four cellular providers: Mercury One-2-One, Orange, Vodafone, and Cellnet have 2.6 million customers, most obtained in the past three years.[9]

7.2 CELLULAR MARKETING PARTNERSHIPS

The cellular industry is shaped by partnerships, each trying to gain market share in the face of new entrants. Cellular is one of the most explosive market segments in telecommunications, adding 17 000 sub-

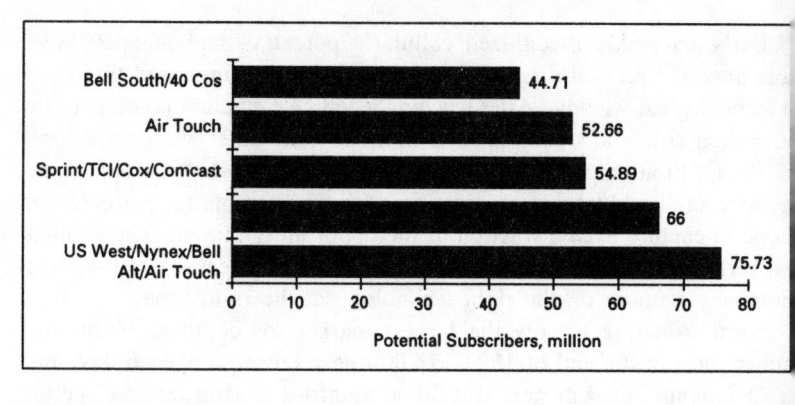

Source: 'Dance of the Cellular Elephants: Grab a Partner' (*International Herald Tribune*, September 16, 1994, 14).

Figure 7.1   Emerging Cellular Market based on Partnerships

scribers per day and over 20 million in total.[10] In fact, the entire next generation of personal communication services (PCS) will be based on wireless technology. The idea is to promote communication between anyone, anywhere at anytime. While wireless communication is not as fast or as clear as fiber optics, it is more convenient.

It was not long ago that the Bells were concerned about cellular because it had the potential of erasing local exchange revenues. The Bells hold monopolies on local exchange services in all but six states and cellular allows alternate service providers to bypass their monopolies. Cellular is not as heavily restricted under the Modified Final Judgment (MFJ) and new players are entering rapidly. The Bells prefer to relinquish monopoly control over the local exchange in return for free competition in inter-exchange and cable television. Now that states are deregulating the local exchange, the Bells are joining cellular partnerships in adjacent service regions.

By developing cellular systems with partner companies, integrated billing, service provision, marketing and customer support can be provided. By adding economies of scale to existing operations, the Bells fend off new competitors in their region. As shown in Figure 7.1, the Bells partnerships are a form of industry collaboration designed to expand established players' existing markets.

The Bells' partnership frenzy was sparked by AT&T's McCaw acquisition. Among the major partnerships:

- US West, Airtouch, Bell Atlantic and Nynex partnership is a massive operation that will cover about one-third of the US population.
- The Sprint, Cox, Comcast, TCI, Wireless Co. partnership is focusing on cable television and on voice and personal communication services. WirelessCo's partners are associated with the worldwide operations of the Teleport alliance that is globalizing the entertainment and information content of its partners. As of October 1994, Sprint Cellular was the fastest growing cellular company in the United States.

It appears that no single player, not even AT&T, can address the national cellular market alone. Partnering is recognized as a mainstream strategy and large players are buying out hundreds of small partners. A micro-partnering strategy employed by the Bells and AT&T expands wireless coverage with a minimum of capital investment. Among those employing micro-partnering are:

- BellSouth, allying with 40 cellular operators in its service region.
- AT&T, joining with Cable and Wireless and hundreds of small cellular providers throughout the US.

Micro-partnering is a win-win scenario, whereby a small company taps the resources of a nationwide network and the large company adds a building block to its network. By acquiring new systems, a uniform service can be offered across multiple states.

Small players are concerned about the intensity of competition and are willing to put an entire business into an alliance. In fact, some providers are lining up to join the most popular alliances because of economies of scale and marketing power.

Motorola has a slightly different tactic in the cellular business through its alliance with the taxi-dispatch company, Nextel Communications. Nextel provides taxi and truck dispatch services via radio that are converted into cellular services. MCI had long thought of allying with Nextel since MCI has virtually no cellular assets. Finally, MCI did not form an alliance with Nextel since it felt the taxi dispatch technology could not be reliably converted into cellular. In fact, no one is sure whether the Nextel technology is viable for cellular but if any partner can help, Motorola can. According to Randy Battat, Corporate VP and GM of Motorola's wireless group,

Motorola has a fundamental belief that [technology] convergence rarely occurs. We see technologies finding their way into different applications.

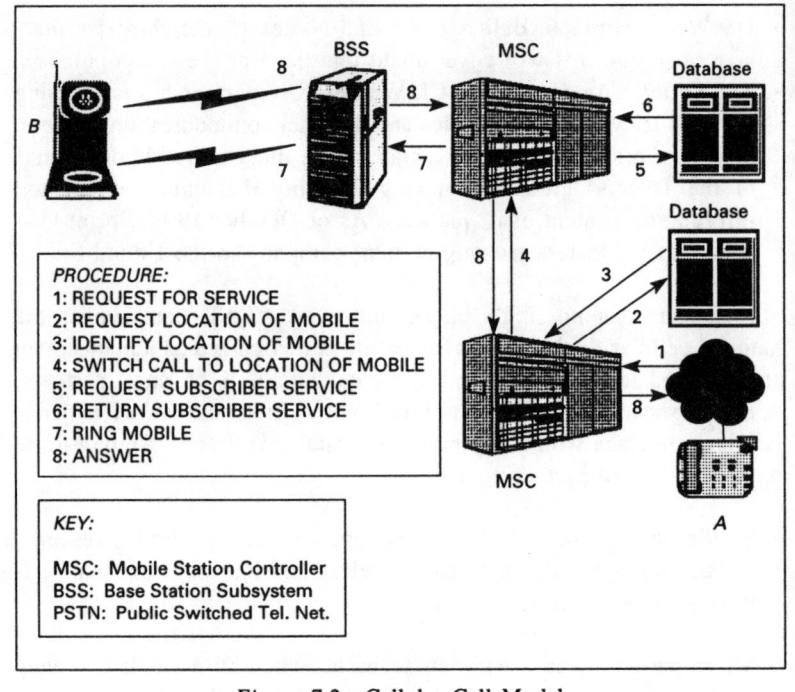

PROCEDURE:
1: REQUEST FOR SERVICE
2: REQUEST LOCATION OF MOBILE
3: IDENTIFY LOCATION OF MOBILE
4: SWITCH CALL TO LOCATION OF MOBILE
5: REQUEST SUBSCRIBER SERVICE
6: RETURN SUBSCRIBER SERVICE
7: RING MOBILE
8: ANSWER

KEY:

MSC: Mobile Station Controller
BSS: Base Station Subsystem
PSTN: Public Switched Tel. Net.

Figure 7.2 Cellular Call Model

By integrating Nextel's technology into Motorola's devices, an entirely new generation of wireless communications devices may be developed. Motorola clearly has the R&D, financial and marketing muscle to bring Nextel's technology into marketable products.

7.3 WIRELESS TECHNOLOGY

The steps involved in making a cellular call are illustrated in Figure 7.2. In Step 1, a Request for Service is made from Calling Party A to the Public Switched Telephone Network (PSTN). In Step 2, the Northern Telecom Mobile Station Controller (MSC) requests verification from the database as to the location of Called Party B. In Step 3, the database responds with the called party's location. In Step 4, the MSC switches the call to the network where the called party is located and verifies the called party's location (Step 5 and 6). In Step 7, the call set-up is requested through to Called Party B and in Step 8, the call is accepted back to Calling Party A. The MSC and BSS technologies

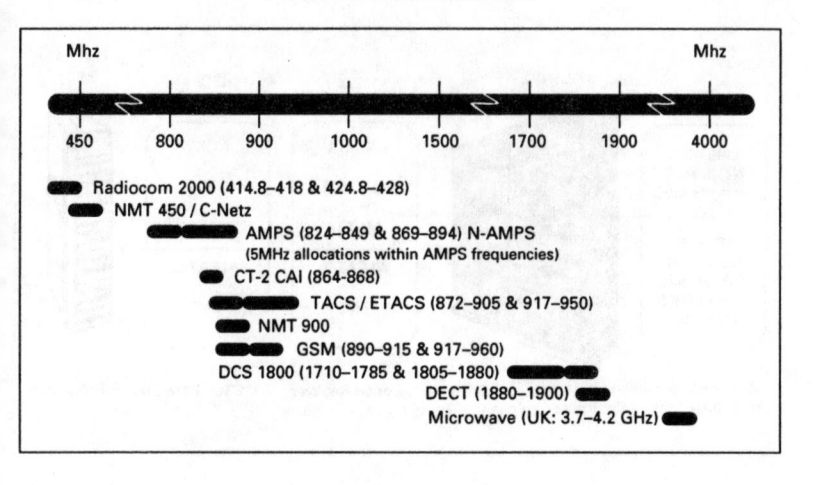

Figure 7.3   The Radio Spectrum

connect the Public Switched Telephone Network to the cellular network.

Cellular and personal communications services (PCS) require precious bandwidth for operation. Cellular operators are constantly seeking more bandwidth to satisfy a greater number of services through wireless devices. Cellular devices rely on whatever frequencies are available or have been allotted by the government. 'Frequency hopping' allows a cellular telephone to tune into whatever frequency is available. If one frequency experiences interference, the phone will automatically hop to another frequency.

The auctioning of available bandwidth to cellular and PCS operators in the US has been a great success. As of January 6, 1995, the Federal Communications Commission (FCC) raised over $2 billion in the first auction. The FCC estimates that it will raise $10 billion after auctioning all saleable bandwidth. There is a total of 27 companies and strategic alliances bidding for 99 licenses in 51 markets. Each market or Major Trading Area (MTA) includes two licenses.[11] The highest bid was placed by McCaw's ALAACR Corporation for $252.7 million, ousting Sprint's WirelessCo for a New York City license. The second highest was in Los Angeles with Pacific Telesis bidding at $183.2 million in the 22nd Round. These licenses will secure the market for cellular service providers in most major US metropolitan areas.

Outside North America, bandwidth is often related to the military. For example, in the Soviet Union and Eastern Europe, the military

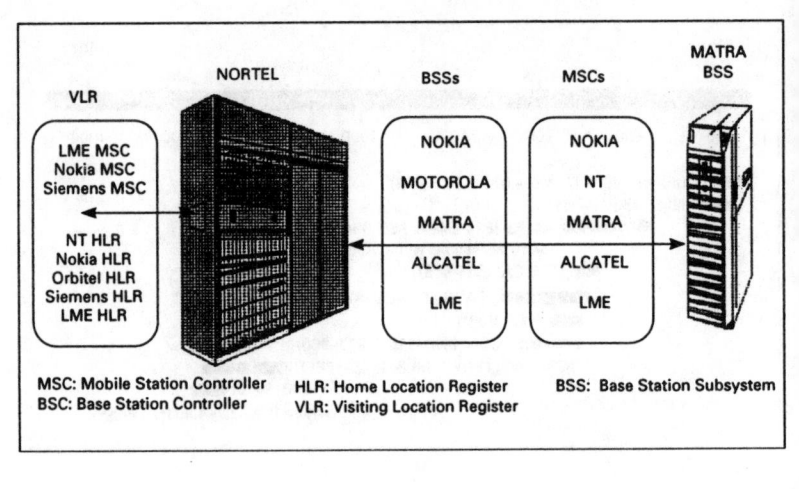

VLR	NORTEL	BSSs	MSCs	MATRA BSS
LME MSC Nokia MSC Siemens MSC		NOKIA MOTOROLA MATRA	NOKIA NT MATRA	
NT HLR Nokia HLR Orbitel HLR Siemens HLR LME HLR		ALCATEL LME	ALCATEL LME	

MSC: Mobile Station Controller HLR: Home Location Register BSS: Base Station Subsystem
BSC: Base Station Controller VLR: Visiting Location Register

Figure 7.4 Nortel–Matra Commitment to Open Interfaces

controls the 900 Mhz frequency that allows Global System Mobile (GSM) telephones to function (see Figure 7.3). In Hungary, the 900 Mhz frequency has been freed, while the Czech and Slovak Republics still wait for their military to free the frequency. The major disadvantage for Eastern Bloc countries without GSM is that travelers from Western Europe cannot use their phones in the East. This deprives the Eastern Bloc phone companies of valuable hard currency phone revenues. Lack of service is also a major inconvenience. In mitigating some of the frequency problems, the French industrial group, Matra has cellular equipment that uses military frequencies (for example its, DCS1800, PCS1900 and Radiocom 2000 technologies).

Northern Telecom teamed up with Matra Communications to develop cellular equipment for markets requiring military frequencies. Matra's military experience in radio and cellular technologies was an especially good match for Northern Telecom's voice switching expertise. As shown in Figure 7.4, both partners used open interfaces that interconnect with other vendors' equipment.

Many benefits were achieved through the Nortel–Matra alliance, among them (i) joint development, (ii) joint testing, (iii) joint marketing, (iv) exchange of know-how, (v) sharing of financial risk, and (vi) accelerating product to market. The parent companies sell equipment separately but call on resources from the alliance to customize marketing programmes. There are a few overlapping products where the partners

compete for the optional systems bundled with cellular. If both partners can fill a need, then a compromise between partners is made on the bid. The combination of complementary products, strong marketing programmes and a well-defined agreement has made this a truly successful partnership.

8 Nortel–Ameritech Service Improvement Program[1]

8.1 INTRODUCTION

Alliances with customers lower a firm's marketing costs, help deliver unique value, and lead to more of each customer's business.[2] The following case study examines Nortel's alliance to build synergies with a customer organization. Nortel responded to a customer's restructuring by analyzing the new organization, accepting new terms, and proactively responding to concerns. The alliance was developed at the VP level and carried the full support of Nortel executives.

In 1984, Nortel won a major equipment bid from Ameritech, taking the business away from AT&T. In 1991, Nortel won almost all of Ameritech's switch business totaling about 4 million of the 5 million lines tendered. The upgrade replaced the AT&T 1ESS and the 1E electromechanical Central Office (CO) switches. The Nortel digital DMS-100 switches replaced the AT&T equipment from 1991 to 1996.[3] Ameritech replaced equipment in the Wisconsin, Illinois, Indiana, Michigan and Ohio service regions. Winning this account significantly increased Nortel's North American presence.

Ameritech's 1992 restructuring programme was designed to reduce costs, improve services, and diversify revenue streams. One area targeted for cost-cutting was customer–supplier relationships. Ameritech relied on AT&T, Siemens and Nortel for most switch purchases. The Supplier Management Program (SMP) was instituted to provide suppliers with a single point of feedback from Ameritech. Feedback was only given *relative* to other suppliers. Each supplier's relative rankings in reliability, cost and responsiveness were presented in a report card (see Figure 8.1).

The reasoning behind the relative rankings was based on an AT&T study. Ray Kordupleski of AT&T found that,

> absolute, raw customer satisfaction scores do not predict changes in market share. Rather, relative customer satisfaction scores and ratios are leading indicators of changes in market share.

- Reliability
- Performance
- Hardware
- Software Delivery
- Workmanship
- Customer Support
- Cost
- Maintenance Cost/Access Line
- Cost of Poor Quality
- Life Cycle Cost
- Pricing
- Supplier Value Added
- Responsiveness
- Order Performance
- Sales Support
- Documentation
- Billing
- Training
- Engineering Complaints
- Product Improvement Initiatives

Figure 8.1   Supplier Report Card

Since Ameritech wanted to effect real changes from suppliers, SMP relayed Ameritech's opinion of how each performed in relation to the others. The results of each assessment were available to all participants of the program.

In 1993, Nortel received its first ratings. Of main concern was software quality on the DMS-100 and the lack of attention specific problems were receiving. Nortel had already lost business from other customers for software quality issues. Nortel's customer support organization in Schaumberg, Illinois, began a 'crusade' to meet Ameritech's demands. In January 1994, Ameritech turned to Nortel President Jean Monty and explained how dire the situation was. A number of high-level meetings followed and Nortel created a strategic alliance called the Ameritech Service Improvement Program (ASIP).

Nortel began the program by listing all the major complaints from Ameritech presented along with their solutions. The major areas of dissatisfaction are shown in Table 8.1. Aiken proposed improvements for each area of dissatisfaction and the potential impact this would have on report card scores.

Table 8.1　Ameritech Service Improvement Program: Areas of
Dissatisfaction, Solutions and Impacts

Major Dissatisfiers	ASIP Fix	ASIP Impact
• Software Reliability	• Design fix	Elimination of related outages
	• No-charge replacements	• Lower switch maint. costs
	• Analyze network to	
	eliminate data risk	• De-risk data management
• Network Performance	• High Performance Team	• 50% reduction in downtime
	• New SW deployment	• CPI Performance
		Improvement
• Responsiveness	• On-site technical support	• Knowledge transfer
	• Address CSRs	• Reduce site outages
• Cost of Ownership	• High Performance Team	• Elimination of Patch Admin.
	• Implement Standard loads	• Reduction in number of loads
• Work Error	• Installation Quality	
	Improvement Programs	• 50% Reduction in Nortel
		work errors
	• Dedicated Application	• Problem focus
	Team	
	• Patch Admin. Automation	• Reduce like-for-like costs
• Major Customers	• Establish Priority Offices	• Ameritech customer focus
• Business Relationship	• Megabid fulfillment	• Single HW/SW Delivery
		point
		• Firm pricing through 2001
	• Bus Process Improve	• Technology Center partnering
		• SW layering & decoupling
	• Evolution of DMS-100	• Services Ready Network

8.2 KEY AREAS OF ASIP

Some of the highlights of the ASIP are described below.

8.2.1 Weekly Executive Telephone Conferences

Ameritech presented Nortel with a list of its problems. This single
point of feedback told Nortel to partner with Ameritech to improve its
relative rankings. Other suppliers were doing the same and the relative amount of suppliers' business with Ameritech would be propor-
tional to SMP ratings. Nortel executives understood the importance of
the rankings and immediately began to alleviate stress points that had
been gnawing at Nortel–Ameritech's relationship.

The weekly executive telephone conferences prioritized Ameritech's
problems in relation to other issues. Nortel executives recognized that
80% of revenues came from 20% of customers. Large customers such

as Ameritech might not require as much attention as small customers under normal circumstances. Small customers do not have the large trained staffs of larger companies and require more attention relative to purchases. Participants in the telephone conferences tried to fit Ameritech's major demands in line with other customer requirements. Investment dollars could be customer-driven by decisions made with the support organization in the conference.

8.2.2 Pro-active Cross Product Teams

The local transmission and switching groups formed cross-product task forces providing the capabilities needed for real responsiveness. Cross-product teams at BNR were put in place to address customer support while others addressed specific product requests from Ameritech. Executive commitment to re-engineering the workflow for particular Ameritech demands was established. Lessons from the Ameritech program were important throughout the Nortel–BNR organizations.

Ameritech was interested in how much Nortel would respond to Ameritech's needs for customized applications. Ameritech also wanted to ensure that DMS-100 would be compatible with standards in Intelligent Networking (IN). For Nortel, the cross-product task forces and external alliances were established to address each of Ameritech's points. Each solution was discussed and Ameritech included concerns about time-frames, delivery, cost, and potential markets. After deciding to develop a new application, business plans were drafted and approved, and the appropriate team commenced development.

The cross-product teams proactively changed switch designs based on Ameritech's assessment and not Nortel's. One of the DMS-100 systems had a feature that had caused outages due to human error. Nothing was faulty with the switch but human operators tended to misuse a function that caused the switch to malfunction. Nortel agreed to redesign the feature at no cost to Ameritech.

Another pro-active effort was made in the reduction of administrative costs. Each time Ameritech wanted new features, different software had to be loaded onto Ameritech's DMS-100 switches. Nortel introduced the *Universal Load* that consisted of all DMS-100 features included in one package, called a 'load.' Nortel billed Ameritech based on the software that Ameritech was actually using. *Universal Loads* reduced the down-time, administration, and on-site technical support associated with separate loading. By eliminating multiple, largely redundant, software loads, a significant reduction in administrative costs was achieved.

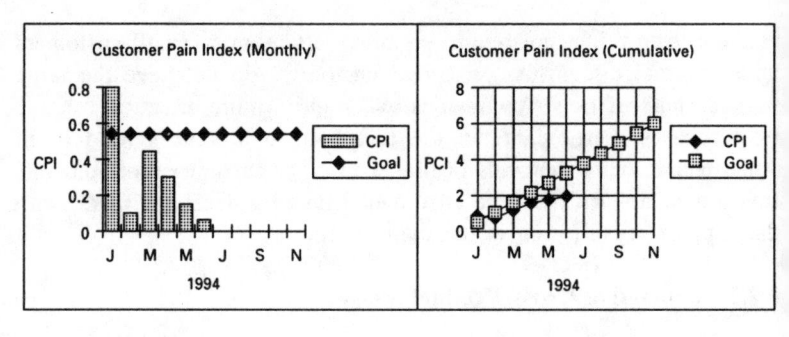

Figure 8.2   Customer Pain Index (Monthly vs. Cumulative)

Customer support was also improved by putting Nortel engineers at Ameritech's Technology Centers. Ten on-site engineers supported two Technology Centers. The engineers provided immediate problem-solving, knowledge transfer and preventive maintenance, keeping the DMS-100 systems in top condition. The value of on-site engineers was to focus on the customer's point of view. Although experience showed that centralizing engineers developed technical synergy, the efforts were often directed towards Nortel's perceived priorities, not Ameritech's priorities. While perhaps more costly from a personnel and travel and living (T&L) expense perspective, the on-site engineers were valuable for allaying Ameritech's problems before they became issues.

8.2.3   Customer Pain Index

The Customer Pain Index (CPI) was established by Nortel's team to assure that its pro-active efforts did not adversely affect Ameritech's service record. While the pro-active measures increased reliability of Ameritech's network in the longer term, outages might occur during the short term. Nortel had to assure Ameritech that proactive maintenance was in the mutual interest of both companies.

For example, if there was an ice storm that disrupted a software distribution, whose fault was it that the software distribution failed and an outage occurred? Using the CPI, all problems were measured in terms of how the end-customer was affected. Irrelevant was whether the problem lay with the service or the equipment provider.

As shown in Figure 8.2, the CPI is based on the worse outage of the week, time when the outage occurred (peak or off-peak), number of lines in/out of service, time to repair outages, and the type of out-

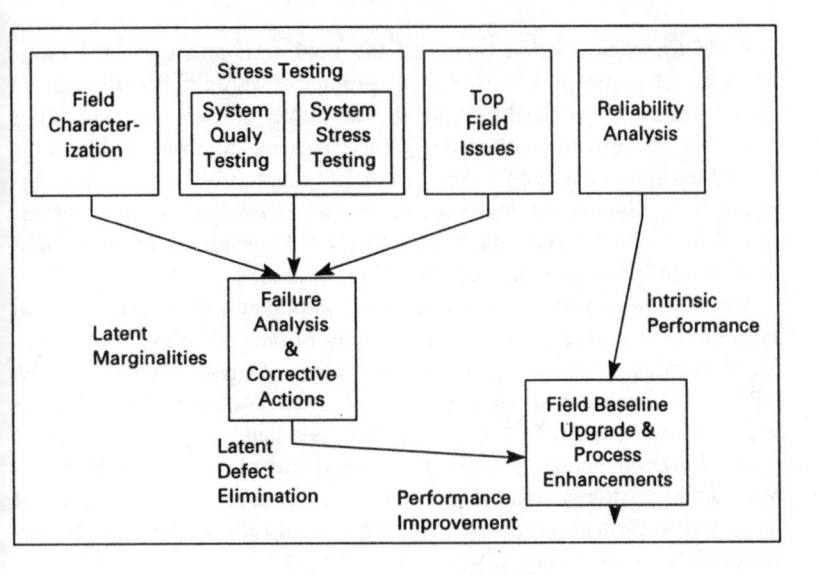

Figure 8.3   Latent Defect Elimination

ages. All factors combined gave a qualitative assessment of how customers were affected through outages. In Figure 8.2, the objective of staying under 0.55% was achieved.

Cumulative CPI controlled preventive maintenance by ensuring that outages remained in check on an annual basis. Pro-active maintenance was always kept within the 0.55% cumulative limit. If major outages occurred, due to weather, for example, there would be less CPI available for pro-active procedures.

8.2.4 Process Engineering to Eliminate Latent Defects

Creating synergies between field technicians, support staff and customers required re-engineering the field process. The re-engineering aimed to reduce mistakes or oversights which required unnecessary additional field visits.

As shown in Figure 8.3, *Latent Defect Elimination* reduced latent problems that might turn into real-time problems. As part of the re-engineering efforts, an attempt was made to predict, analyze, and schedule the elimination of latent defects. Removing problems before they occurred would minimize impact on the CPI. The process engineering chart shown in Figure 8.3 illustrates the essential process elements that each field engineer would have to address in every field visit.

Field Characterization preceded the field visit and informed engineers about latent problems. Latent problems weren't directly visible to a technician but might occur in the future or contribute to other problems. A proven methodology for checking common field issues for all customers helped avoid revisits. Latent problems were diagnosed by analyzing the statistics of processor outages, switch events, link failures, and field data. Correcting latent problems on each field visit would eventually reduce recurring situations.

Stress Testing was used to exercise equipment and determine what failures occur during peak periods (usually Monday–Friday, 8am–5pm). Since failures during the peak periods were the greatest enemy of the CPI, stress testing was an important process. *System Quality Testing* was performed at the factory in a system test bed using regression test plans. *Environmental Stress Testing* characterized the switch performance under customer conditions. For example, a processor reset might be added to protect against continuing system failure after power was restored from an outage.

Customer Top Field Issues identified the 30 top issues that had already been solved. Field engineers used these as a guideline in determining what the problems at different sites were.

Failure Analysis and Corrective Actions used all of the data just described to eliminate latent defects. Latent Defect Elimination initially required increased staff levels, new processes, increased problem tracking and new software. Latent Defect Elimination contributed to short-term outages measured against the Cumulative CPI that assured rationality in pro-active maintenance.

Reliability Analysis calculated the average failure rate for processors, features and lines, and determined when replacements were needed. This method was analagous to Mean Time Between Failure (MTBF) predictions. System unavailability schedules were determined and the most appropriate times for upgrades were scheduled. Obviously, it was better to upgrade during off-peak periods rather than busy day periods.

Field Baseline Upgrade and Process Enhancements comprised the actual field operations including upgrades and replacements. These processes tracked the length of an outage during an upgrade.

The outcome of the entire field process re-engineering effort was a significant improvement in the Ameritech network as a whole.

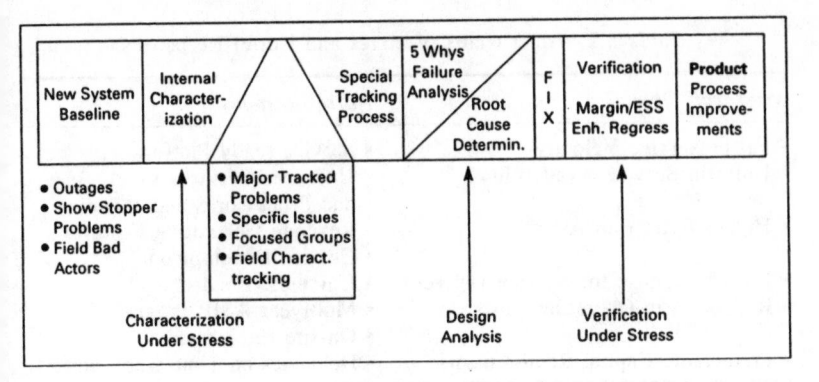

Figure 8.4   Software Quality Improvement

8.2.5   Process Re-engineering to Improve Software Quality

Figure 8.4 illustrates ASIP's team focus for reducing overall software problems at Ameritech. The process began by establishing a *New System Baseline* for tracking outages, stopper problems (problems that stop service) and bad field actors (people or objects). The *New System Baseline* is developed by ASIP's Engineering Design Analysis Team.

Internal Characterization attempted to characterize the switch's stress performance. Functions, stresses and performance margins were calculated. The Product Conformance Test Team composed of both the Product Integrity, Product Assurance and Component Engineering groups tracked major known problems. The team also focused on specific issues and field characteristics. Teams were familiar with the customer and the specific problems of that customer. They were equipped with tools required to track down specific problems through historical and real-time data. For each problem there were *5 Whys* for failure occurrence. The *Root Cause* was determined and a *Fix* was implemented. *Verification* was performed using margins and *Statistical Regression* in determining the robustness of the system during fluctuating conditions.

The *Verification Under Stress* was performed by the Verification/ Technical Assistance and Support (TAS) Team. The team was composed of three groups: on-site field engineers, a small dedicated TAS group and manufacturing and operations. The end results of team efforts were product and process improvements.

It wasn't just a band-aid or quick fix. Though the new way of life required a new, higher level of support, the new processes ensured

Table 8.2   Ameritech Objectives and Nortel Responses

Ameritech Objective	Nortel Response
• Faster Service Velocity	• Service-ready Platform
• Uniform Service Availability	• Universal Services Load and Processor Standardization
• Higher Return on Assets	• Revenue Generating Features
	• Custom Development
• Lower Expense for Service Delivery	• Universal Loads
• Reduction in Operating Costs	• Multiyear ASIP Program
	• On-site Engineers
• Predictable Capital Requirements	• Deliveries on Time with Forecast

that field jobs were done correctly the first time around. Each field process integrated the centralized support organization and the on-site engineers.

A summary of Ameritech's objectives and Nortel's responses is given in Table 8.2. The research points to a need for synergy-building process flows between customers and suppliers such as those in the Ameritech Service Improvement Program. Especially important are direct linkages between customer and supplier groups for tracking problems, relaying concerns, and providing feedback. A Nortel champion created ASIP and became a way of life dictated by the customer's demands. Synergies continue to grow and this alliance is more important than ever.

Has Ameritech's restructuring helped? According to financial reports it has. Ameritech's second quarter of 1994 was the strongest in the company's history with earnings rising over 14% to $446 million from $389 million one year earlier. Revenues rose 6.6% to $3.15 billion from $2.95 billion.[4] The growth was fueled by increasing network usage with access minutes up 7.9%. Ground-based access lines in service grew 2.5 million to 17.9 million. It appears that Ameritech is on-track with its business reorganization and that Nortel has become an important partner in that success.

9 R&D Consortia

9.1 GLOBAL SATELLITE CONSORTIA

These satellites have a great potential to make the entire world economy more productive, and will make it easier and cheaper to solve communications problems in less-developed countries (FCC Chairman, Reed Hundt).[1]

You have to spend years building the system without getting a dollar of revenue... You have to stick your money into firecrackers, launch them, and hope it all goes right (Ron Mario, President of Comsat Mobile Communications, commenting on expansion plans).[2]

It is a little scary to think that TRW has been in the satellite business for 35 years, and we have put up just 200 satellites in all that time (TRW President, Edsel Dunford).[3]

Distribution will be key... They [satellite consortia] are going to need a local marketing presence, since they will literally have to be able to sell everywhere (Barry Goodstadt, consultant to EDS Corp).[4]

The market for global wireless communications is being formed by consortia that are propelling the forces of globalization. Major contenders in this emerging market use the forces of globalization to create demand for standard, globalized telecommunication services. While existing voice service providers such AT&T, Sprint and MCI offer standardized voice services from most major countries, there are many areas of the world where such service is not available.

Wired services such as AT&T's WorldPhone require that callers use a land-based telephone. This requires a certain, albeit minimal knowledge of the local telecommunications service. While this knowledge is minimal, it can be difficult to acquire just after arriving in a foreign country. Different coins, dial tones, numbering plans, languages, busy signals, and ringing tones cause confusion when dialing toll-free access numbers. For example, in the Czech Republic, after a number is dialed, the telephone makes a tone indicating the call is being connected. This tone is similar to the busy signal in North America and

most North American callers think they are getting a busy signal and hang up.

Global satellite systems will allow calls from anywhere in the world to bypass the local telecommunications system. Once they are widely deployed, satellite systems may change the face of the telecommunications industry. Countries will have to collect their service fees through wireline access charges.

9.1.1 The Service Concept

The main service advantage of global systems is the uniformity of service for the entire world. Each local service provider is bypassed with the customer dialing directly into the satellite system. Billing, operator services, enhanced services, and language are entirely coordinated from one company. Whether a customer is in Fiji or India, the service is exactly the same, i.e. the user dials and completes calls in the same way. The simplicity and quality of worldwide communication services should be a boon to the ubiquity of global communications services.

The consortia mitigate the multi-billion dollar financial risk that each system demands. In order to recoup costs, providers are expected to price access time at $3.00 to $4.00 per minute. This is at least 3–4 times the price of standard cellular telephony in the US and twice the price of European cellular telephony.

In order to find payback, the marketing plans of each of the consortia call for $1–2 billion in revenues by the year 2001. Whether these systems can capture subscribers who are willing to pay high tariffs, or how many will actually subscribe is uncertain. Most marketing plans call for high-end business users to be the initial target customers. High-end users are those that travel extensively and need satellite systems where cellular telephony is unavailable. Customers may also seek the simplicity of service. Perhaps in the year 2000, several hundred thousand business users will comunicate via global satellite systems, but probably not the million subscribers targeted in the marketing plans.

In finding more subscribers, marketing plans rely on users from developing countries where good communications services are not available. Hundreds of millions of subscribers are in this category but the tariffs may be too high to attract them. If each consortia could capture 0.06% of the world's population by the year 2002, revenue goals would be met.

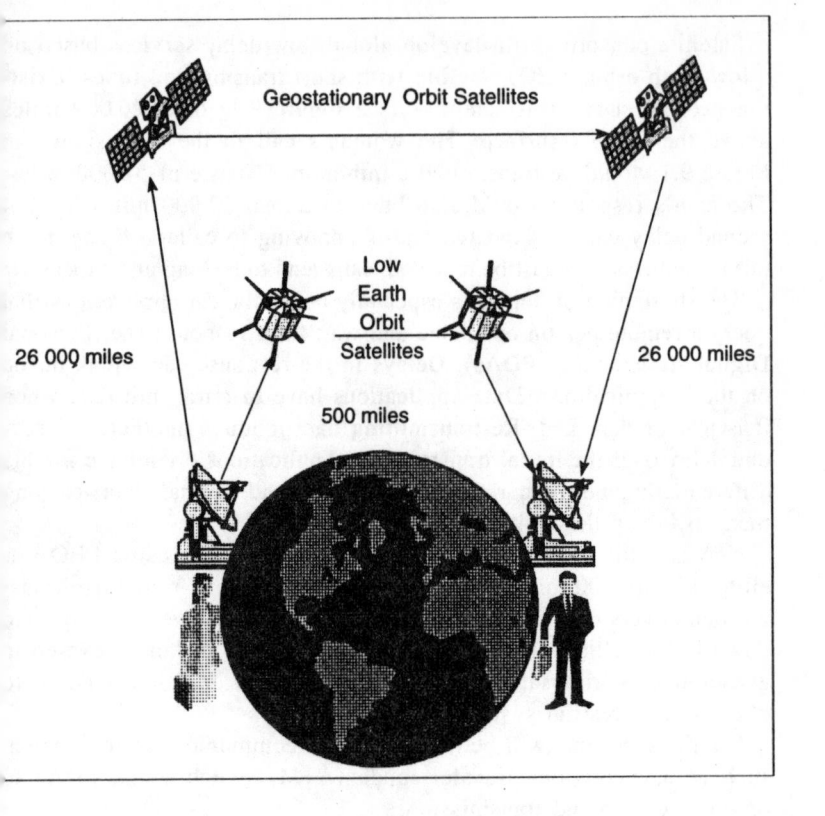

Figure 9.1   Comparison of Satellite Systems

9.1.2   Achieving the Technology

Consortia are formed to mitigate the huge financial and technical risks associated with the global satellite technology. Satellite communications has long been a means for worldwide communications but services have traditionally suffered from poor voice and transmission quality. Voice transmitted via satellite experiences echoes and delays that interfere with conversations and cause poor performance in interactive applications. The emerging satellite consortia will deliver higher quality satellite service.

Satellite consortia will develop global, low-delay services based on a low-earth-orbit (LEO) satellite with short transmission times. Existing geostationary orbit satellites (see Figure 9.1) orbit 26 000 miles above the Earth's surface. The woman's call to the man shown in Figure 9.1 would be transmitted a minimum distance of 52 000 miles. The man's response would also have to transit 52 000 miles. A 2–4 second delay can be expected and is annoying to callers. Since much of the conversation must be repeated, calls tend to be long and expensive.

The shortening of delays is especially beneficial for applications that query a remote person or device and wait for a response (i.e. Personal Digital Assistants or PDAs). Delays in the response can wreak havoc on these applications. Data applications have to retransmit data when it is lost or damaged. Re-transmitting data requires another 2–4 second delay over the initial transmission. Applications often have trouble differentiating between re-transmitted data and normal data, causing them to fail in these situations.

New satellite systems will have much lower delays using LEO satellites at only 500 miles above the Earth's surface. A round trip transmission covers only 1000 miles plus the distance between the up- and down-link satellites. This is only a fraction of the distance covered in geostationary orbit satellite systems and delays are almost equal to fiber optic terrestrial systems.

Satellites systems will be integrated into communications equipment such as asynchronous transfer mode (ATM) switches and PDAs to optimize end-to-end transmission.

While in theory, the satellite communication system is a good idea, such a project is massive and requires expertise from a host of top space and telecommunications companies. Putting hundreds of satellites into orbit and making them communicate effectively with ground stations is a significant human feat. It is in the same league as the space station and Star Wars.

The technology of these consortia borrows heavily from Star Wars and significant technological barriers exist. For one, ground-based communication systems have never been developed to deal with so many satellites. Even at Colorado-based North American Aerospace Defense Command (Norad), where most satellites are tracked, no more than 350 satellites are tracked by the ground station at any one time. The founders of these new massive systems are making bets that their systems can out perform anything in existence.

Microsoft's consortium aims to put over 800 satellites into orbit, each acting as a 'brilliant pebble' to pick up ground-based transmis-

sions. The ground-based transmissions will switch calls from one 'brilliant pebble' to another until the call reaches its final destination.

9.1.3 Cross-Section of the Consortia

The array of strategic consortia that are betting on satellite technology as a next generation of communications is daunting. Most analysts do not believe that all can survive and some consolidation may occur. There are seven consortia, and each is trying to raise necessary funding by acquiring new partners.

Iridium

Motorola's Iridium consortium has been the most successful by raising $1.6 billion in funding. Iridium was just a dream five years ago when Motorola announced the project. Now, Iridium has almost 50 partners with total funding expected to reach $3.37 billion by the year 2002. Iridium will have launched 66 satellites in a low earth orbit 500 miles above the Earth's surface.

   Iridium's partners have been chosen to either: (a) provide marketing and technical services in a geographic region or (b) develop the technologies required to make the project a reality. Those partners that fit in category (a) include Motorola, BCE Mobile Communications, Sprint, Italy's STET, Thailand's United Communications Corp., Venezuela's Muidiri Investments BVI Ltd., Germany's Vebacom, Japan's Daini Denden & Kyocera, Sony, Mitsubishi and Mitsui, Saudi Arabia's Mawadari Group, South America's Nepari Group, Korea's Korean Mobile Communications, and India's Motorola India Communications. Those partners that fit into category (b) are Motorola, Lockheed, and Raytheon. The diverse mix of partners will make the pursuit of common goals a management feat in itself.

Globalstar

A system called Globalstar LP (see Figure 9.2) is being formed by Loral Communications, Qualcomm, AirTouch Communications, France's Alcatel–Alsthom, South Korea's Hyundai Electronics & DaCom, Germany's DASA subsidiary of Daimler-Benz, England's Vodaphone and Italy's Alena Spazio. The Loral plans are more modest than Iridium with 48 satellites costing $1.8 billion. It relies heavily on telephone systems in existence both before and after the launch of satellites.

   Globalstar's marketing plan calls for 2.7 million subscribers by 2002

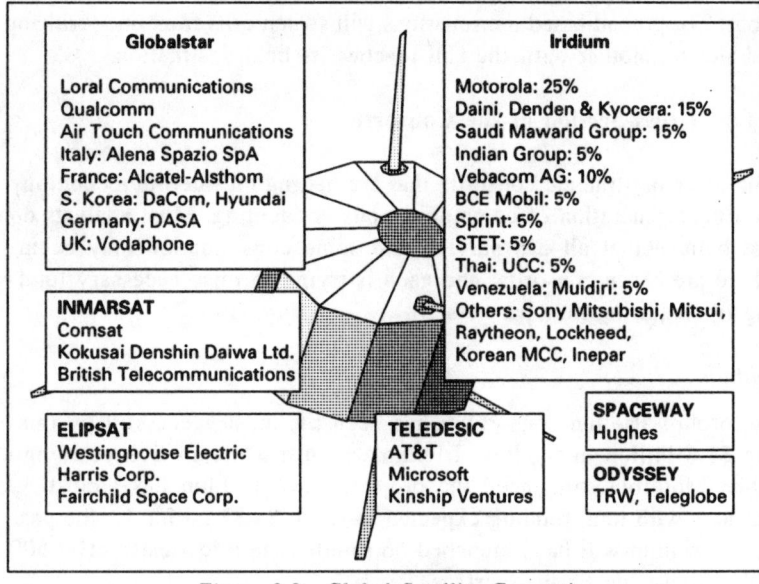

Figure 9.2   Global Satellite Consortia

with revenues of $1.6 billion. The pricing structure for Globalstar is more modest than other consortia with calls costing $0.65/minute. To recoup costs, the subscriber base must increase to 16 million by the year 2012. Partners in the alliance have been carefully chosen for their ability to both invest in and sell the services.

INMARSAT

The most controversial consortium is the International Maritime Satellite Organization (INMARSAT), a 71 nation consortium that is 25%-owned by US Comsat. INMARSAT will start the INMARSAT-P network catering to commercial markets and making the best use of existing satellite systems.

INMARSAT's satellite systems have been funded either through the US or other government organizations. Its Comsat partner is represented in international treaties and has received government assistance through funding, tax breaks and incentives. INMARSAT still remains the sole provider of easily accessible worldwide satellite communications. It is unclear how much INMARSAT's headstart is worth to emerging, privately-funded operators.

INMARSAT now offers a telephone costing $10 000–$15 000 that

can be used anywhere in the world. It's famous debut was during CNN's coverage of US bombing in the Gulf War. CNN used the INMARSAT telephone to broadcast pictures of US bombing from a Baghdad hotel. As new products enter the market, INMARSAT telephones will come down to $1000–$2500.

In the year 2000, INMARSAT plans to have 12 satellites at a total cost of $2.6 billion. It will continue to be a lower-end service provider relying on the 12 satellites. The compound revenues from INMARSAT's 45 000 subscribers from now until the year 2000 make this consortia one of the most financially promising.

Teledesic

One of the most exciting consortia is Teledesic planned by Bill Gates of Microsoft and Craig McCaw of AT&T's McCaw Cellular.[5] Gates and McCaw plan to launch 840 satellites at a 435 mile orbit at a cost of $9 billion. The system is three times Iridium's cost and revenue projections include a wide range of telecommunications services.

Teledesic can only be profitable if an entire generation of PDAs, telephony and computer communications can be integrated into the Teledesic communications system. AT&T's strategy of bringing equipment manufacturers and software developers onto its network will probably play a role in investing in Teledesic. It must use partners to integrate systems into Teledesic. This is similar to AT&T Worldworx and WorldPartners programmes that rely on AT&T switching equipment. Microsoft may have the technical and marketing power to engage the software development community into Teledesic. Whether AT&T and Microsoft can together, invest in and perform one of the greatest technological feats ever, remains to be seen.

Others

Additional consortia include TRW's Odyssey, Westinghouse Electric, Harris Corp. and Fairchild's Space Corp.'s Elipsat and Hughes Space Systems' Spaceway projects. These consortia have been largely planned with advanced space research firms. Defense contractors are rapidly making the transition into civilian technology and consortia may be the right vehicle.

Next generation satellite systems will be an exciting area for development and marketing via strategic alliances. Advancements in management can be expected considering the feat of managing multiple non-controlling partners on a massive global project. The evolution of

this market may be indicative of future markets in the 22nd century. The complexity and cost of huge projects combined with intense rivalry may make consortia shapers of future industries.

Satellite consortia may be the true herald of the space age, ushering in new ways of thinking about Earth-based communications. For now, the best technical bets are those with experience in Star Wars, and the best marketing bets are those with locally sensitive operations. Since this is still a fractionalized array of alliances, the ultimate emergence of a leader will depend on the benefit that each consortium partner receives. For now, it is all a dream and cash must be lent against promises.

9.2 BELLCORE

This is Bellcore's last chance (a senior White House Aid).

Everyone knows that cooperatives are not very efficient (a Bell Operating Company executive).

I'll always believe that Bellcore should play a significant role in the process that takes place as America meets the global challenges of the 21st Century. I also think that relief from the Modified Final Judgment is crucial to this process. Just one of the major changes that must take place in the policy and regulation arena if the National Information Infrastructure is to be built efficiently and realize its true potential . . . Bellcore believes its skills are crucial to this process. We are building the capabilities that are necessary to fulfill this role. I believe Bellcore can earn the right to contribute in all areas of the industry (George Heilmeier, CEO of Bellcore).

Bellcore was established during the 1984 breakup as a centralized R&D facility for the Baby Bells. Bellcore's mission was to provide centralized monitoring of network reliability, equipment procurement and equipment reliability. Its four divisions are (i) Applied Research, performing basic research; (ii) Operations Technology, supporting implementation of new services and technology; (iii) Software Technology and Systems, supporting development of software-based systems; and (iv) Network Technology, designing network technology. The Software Technology division has been one of the most successful since it can produce software, not considered a manufacturing activity.

Bellcore has a Board of Directors with seven members, each repre-

Table 9.1   Voting and Non-Voting Members of Bellcore

Voting Members (Bellcore Client Co.s)	Non-voting Members
Ameritech	SNET
Bell Atlantic	Cincinnati Bell
NYNEX	
Bell South	
Pacific Bell	
Southwestern Bell	
US West	

sentative of one voting member. Table 9.1 lists the seven voting and two non-voting members of Bellcore. Although the non-voting members, SNET and Cincinnati Bell, were Baby Bells which AT&T did not control under the AT&T Bell System, they joined Bellcore.

With the Information Superhighway a growing reality, it is unclear how Bellcore will fit in. Bellcore's seven voting members have cut back on their R&D funding and have forced Bellcore's CEO, George Heilmeier, to trim budgets and staff. Heilmeier successfully reduced administrative costs by 16% without affecting technical staff.[6] Bellcore continues its programme of being more efficient and finding new roles for itself as the telecommunications industry evolves. For example, Bellcore was chosen to be the North American Numbering Plan Administrator (NANPA). In this role Bellcore oversees allocation of numbers and changes required to the telephone numbering system. Heilmeier is responding to members' demands and set the agenda shown in Figure 9.3.

The Baby Bells are changing their R&D strategies to accommodate fast-moving technologies in an increasingly competitive environment.[7] Spinning off Bellcore into a separate company might make more effective use of its $1.1 billion in annual member funding. Not only have the Baby Bells questioned Bellcore, but so have telephone ratepayers who are subsidizing the central laboratory. Non-Bellcore members support Bellcore by being R&D partners that participate in certain projects (for a complete listing of all Bellcore alliance partners, refer to Appendix 3). But non-Bellcore members generally oppose national projects given to Bellcore since they have little management input into Bellcore.

Clinton officials believe Bellcore is the best organization to develop open standards for interoperability of telecommunications technologies.[8] As long as Clinton is in power, Bellcore's future is safe. Vice President Al Gore supports Bellcore as a centralized laboratory for the creation

- *Set Strategic Direction*: The Board of Directors has chosen seven priority programmes for Bellcore.
- *Pare Bureaucracy*: 20% of the controller's group has been downsized through attrition. More cuts are to follow.
- *Speed up Decision Making*: Researchers will recommend actions, not just follow directives.
- *Improve Quality*: Total Quality Management (TQM) is emphasized, including training for Quality Circles.
- *Increase Information Sciences Research*: Work in object-oriented computing, multimedia, fuzzy logic, etc. has been increased.

Source: Smith, E. and Coy, P., 'Pumping up the Baby Bells' R&D Arm' (*Science and Technology*, August 5, 1991, 68).

Figure 9.3   Heilmeier's Game Plan for Bellcore

of open technical standards of the Information Superhighway. The Courts, Congress and the FCC have made regulatory rulings favoring the Bells in the 1992 Cable Act, opposing the cable–telco cross-ownership ban, and favoring video dialtone. The Bells probably will not jeopardize the deregulatory trend by eliminating Bellcore.

Bellcore's main strategic thrust appears to be in equipment R&D and law permitting, in manufacturing. If the line of business restriction banning equipment manufacture is lifted, Bellcore could manufacture its own equipment. Bellcore could sell local exchange equipment to new competitors after the local exchange market is de-monopolized. Bellcore's technical core competencies include Integrated Services Digital Network (ISDN), Switched Multimegabit Data Service (SMDS), Asynchronous Transfer Mode (ATM) and Synchronous Optical Network (SONET).

Advanced Intelligent Networking/Intelligent Networking (AIN/IN) is an R&D field in which Bellcore has had particular success. AIN/IN is mainly a software product and although the MFJ's line of business restrictions do not allow Bellcore to manufacture hardware, there are no restrictions on software. The Bells AIN/IN strategy is in being as hardware-independent as possible and developing software that can be used on any vendor's switch. AIN/IN products are not 'manufactured' and AIN/IN software has become one of Bellcore's core competencies. Bellcore Client Company, Bell Atlantic, produced the highly competitive Intelligent Services Computing Platform (ISCP) through Bellcore R&D. Bell Atlantic now has a significant lead over the competition in AIN/IN technology. In 1993, Sprint signed a two year agreement to

participate in the AIN/IN programme and additional carriers are buying into the programme.

9.2.1 Increasing Project Participation

One of the major tasks of a consortium is to attract participation in sponsored projects. Only through active and committed participation of members can an R&D consortium survive. The Bellcore budgeting programme is designed to increase the participation of Bellcore members without more funding. Based on research done by the Task Force on Bellcore Effectiveness,[9] Bellcore researchers developed a 0–1 non-linear programming algorithm for project funding. The algorithm enables Bellcore Client Companies (BCC) to share costs optimally across different projects, each receiving maximum R&D.

In 1991, there were 1046 projects (a project is the smallest unit of sale to a BCC). Projects generally run for one fiscal year but may start in the middle of a year. Work that takes place over several years is linked by a dependency relationship so that participants share the cost of the project over its entire lifespan. Previously, if a BCC bought into a project before completion, it had to pay for all dependent projects.

The methodology developed by the Task Force on Bellcore Effectiveness was directed at elective projects. When a BCC decides to buy into an additional project, it must pay a buy-in fee. If the project is new, this money does not go to Bellcore. It goes to the BCCs who originally funded the project. Every buy-in creates a debit to the buy-in BCC and credits the originally-funding BCCs.

Figures 9.4 and 9.5 illustrate how this methodology works. The dependencies are shown in both figures through the arrows. D and E (1990 and 1989) are providers to C (1991); B (1989) is a provider to B (1991): A (1989) is a provider to A (1991). The P indicates prior year participations and 1991 participations in the initial view.

The 1991 participations (Figure 9.4) show that BCC1 participated in Project A, BCC2 participated in Project B and BCC3 participated in Project C. The $200 000 represents the initial buy-in fee for each of the projects. If BCC3 wants to participate in Project C in 1991, it must pay the buy-in fee and it must buy-in to Project D. The $115 000 consist of $100 000, 1990 price; $5000, interest for one year late payment; and $10 000, risk fee contingent on the project's success. BCC3 must pay the $115 000 which goes to BCC1 which is no longer participating in Project C. The net bill for 1991 is $85 000, $200 000 and $315 000 for BCC1, BCC2 and BCC3, respectively. There is

Project Number	Year	Price $K	1991 Participants			1991 Bill $K		
			BCC1	BCC2	BCC3	BCC1	BCC2	BCC3
A	91	200	P			200		
B	91	200		P			200	
C	91	200			P			200
			Prior Year Participants			**Bill for Prior Years**		
D	90	100	P		X	–115		115
E	89	100			P			
B	89	100		P				
A	89	100	P					
					Net Bill	85	200	315

Source: Hoadley, B., Katz, P. and Sadrian, A., 'Improving the Utility of the Bellcore Consortium' (*Interface*, 23, January–February 1993, 31).

Figure 9.4   Initial View of the Budget

Project Number	Year	Price $K	1991 Participations			1991 Bill $K		
			BCC1	BCC2	BCC3	BCC1	BCC2	BCC3
A	91	100	P	P*		100	100	
B	91	100		P	P*		100	100
C	91	100	P		P	100		100
			Prior Year Participants			**Bill for Prior Years**		
D	90	100	P		X	–115		115
E	89	100	X*		P	121		–121
B	89	100		P	X*		–121	121
A	89	100	P	X*		–121	121	
					Net Bill	85	200	315

Source: Hoadley, B., Katz, P. and Sadrian, A., 'Improving the Utility of the Bellcore Consortium' (*Interface*, 23, January–February 1993).

Figure 9.5   Increased Participational View of the Budget

some inflexibility in this approach when project participation is changed.

In the Increased Participational View (Figure 9.5) of the 1991 budget, the P*s are the added participations and the X*s are the required, prior year buy-ins. For 1991, the new price is $100 000 (instead of $200 000) because participation has doubled. BCC1 has to pay $121 000 to buy-in to E for 1989; $100 000 of this is the 1988 price, $10 000 is risk fee and $11 000 is two years' worth of interest. In this view, BCC1 has continued its participation in Project C. BCC3 can participate in both Project B and C and BCC2 can participate in both Project A and B. The net bills for the year are the same while participation has doubled.

This methodology has been implemented at Bellcore in the face of cost-cutting measures. In 1991, there were 143 elective projects eligible for increased participation. The total Bellcore cost was $14 million or 12% of the budget. The average participation of the BCCs increased from 3.7 to 4.9 projects: an increase of 30%. The total buy-in prices of these projects was $52.6 million, but the net bill was the same.[10] The additional deliverables received by the various BCCs included software systems, technology and new service analyses.

Increased flexibility in project participation allows members with diverse needs to participate in R&D. This methodology has been used at the Micro-electronics and Computer Technology Corporation (MCC) where average participation increased from 6.1 to 8.9 members per project. MCC projects range from electronic packaging to advanced neural networking. The R&D funding methodology described here is a useful lesson for all joint R&D organizations.

10 Joint Development Alliances

10.1 NETWORK MANAGEMENT SYSTEM ALLIANCE

In the following case, synergies were built between customers and a third party software developer. As an equipment supplier found its customer becoming reliant on the third party software, it was forced into a partnership. After the partnership was established, management focused on synergy building, eliminating duplication, reducing not-invented-here and promoting communication. (The names of the individuals and companies have been changed to protect their identities.)

QuickTel was formed in 1990 by Larry Turnkey, an ex-BigComm employee to develop software which, in Turnkey's mind, filled a gap. QuickTel would develop additional software modules for the BigComm network management system (NMS) that BigComm had not yet developed.

NMS was used by operators to control large telecommunications networks. It ran on a Sun Microsystems workstation that displayed graphical diagrams of the network, reported trouble spots, and assisted operators in locating problems. NMS allowed operators to change on-switch service data and correct communications errors. It allowed the network to be fixed and managed in real-time.

Some customers had needs for optional tools that could be purchased in addition to the base system. Customers could order any number of optional tools depending on the size of their network and other requirements. QuickTel's *Planning, Statistics, Accounting*, and *Analysis* tools added planning, statistical, accounting and analysis features to NMS. Since the accounting tool is used for billing, it is one of the most important network tools. While BigComm had an accounting tool, it was not yet fully integrated into the NMS system. Some customers had never used BigComm's accounting system and had only considered QuickTel's solution. Turnkey recognized the need for such tools on the NMS system and pre-empted BigComm's introduction of its tools.

Although BigComm could eventually develop the missing systems, QuickTel had a head start. QuickTel used its highly focused, rapid development team and its entrepreneurial drive to oust BigComm's slower more methodical development efforts. BigComm saw these tools

as being peripheral to the overall scheme of development and continued NMS development along original lines. QuickTel focused its motivation and ousted BigComm in satisfying customer requests for the *Accounting* tool. QuickTel released the new software ahead of BigComm's release and started to persuade customers that QuickTel's solution was ready and better. QuickTel sold directly to BigComm's customers and offered attractive training packages.

QuickTel was soon bombarding customers with offers of new software, free trials, demonstrations and training. Customers were interested in QuickTel's additional NMS features since none of BigComm's features had yet been released. R&D staffs of large customers were eager to trial features with QuickTel prior to general release.

As orders for QuickTel NMS started to ring up, Turnkey turned to BigComm. He wanted an alliance that would not only integrate his tools directly into NMS but would allow him to sell through BigComm's channels.

BigComm had its own product groups focusing on these tools, but these teams were assisting important product groups on other parts of the NMS system. Management was unwilling to acknowledge the QuickTel development efforts since the software was internally contracted for development. Management had little incentive to recognize QuickTel since internal budgets reflected planned upstream activities. There were definitely no internal or external synergies being developed in regards to the *Accounting* tool.

Not long thereafter, a few customers got confused as to whom they should contact concerning support for QuickTel's NMS tools. If a problem arose, was the problem in BigComm's NMS or QuickTel's NMS? If customers wanted BigComm's NMS tools training, could they get the QuickTel NMS training during the BigComm NMS training or vice-versa? What was BigComm's plan on porting the old tools to interwork with the new tools?

Customers were demanding answers, solutions and guarantees but BigComm was only vaguely familiar with QuickTel and its products. How could customers know about BigComm's NMS system and have NMS tools that BigComm didn't know about? Now, BigComm could no longer ignore the QuickTel Corporation and Larry Turnkey was given an appointment.

Not long thereafter, BigComm announced its alliance with QuickTel and customers were relieved. They were satisfied to see BigComm working together with the supplier of their software. BigComm promptly informed customers that the new QuickTel tools were supported and would be available directly from BigComm. The tools were integrated

into NMS by using available resources from the original internal development groups. Most of the internal product groups were reassigned to more pressing activities.

Perhaps BigComm should have acquired QuickTel early-on in the game and subsumed the QuickTel developers directly into BigComm's development team. Acquisition might have gotten a swifter and more unified evolution of NMS out to customers. On the other hand, it is easy to see in retrospect that an acquisition would have been smart. At the time, no one was convinced of the merit of QuickTel's product. Customers had to convince their trusted supplier that this was an important part of NMS and that QuickTel had the entrepreneurial drive to deliver.

The BigComm–QuickTel alliance shows how customers can drive alliances and force synergy building. QuickTel was able to give customers a solution independently of BigComm. BigComm had always chosen a go-it-alone approach to NMS, turning a blind eye to QuickTel. While this might have worked had there not been an alternative for customers, the customers would have suffered through lack of development synergies. Instead, external synergies were developed between BigComm, QuickTel and customers. In the end this alliance has been a win-win deal for all involved and BigComm's NMS system continues to be one of the best in the industry.

10.2   ADVANCED INTELLIGENT NETWORKING (AIN) ALLIANCES

Equipment makers are now working hand-in-hand with customers and competitors in rival industries. Inter-corporate synergies are being developed in a business where collaboration means survival.

Advanced Intelligent Networking/Intelligent Networking (AIN/IN) is a telecommunications market that equipment manufacturers are capturing through strategic alliances. The market for intelligent network applications is forecast to grow from $475 million in 1994 to $1.3 billion in 1997.[1] Strategic alliances are used for industry collaboration, standard-setting and joint R&D. Competition between telecommunications equipment manufacturers, on the one hand, and computer equipment manufacturers, on the other, shapes the market in a new way. The computer and telecommunications industries are merging and the shape of the new industry is based on competition, appropriability regimes, and alliances.

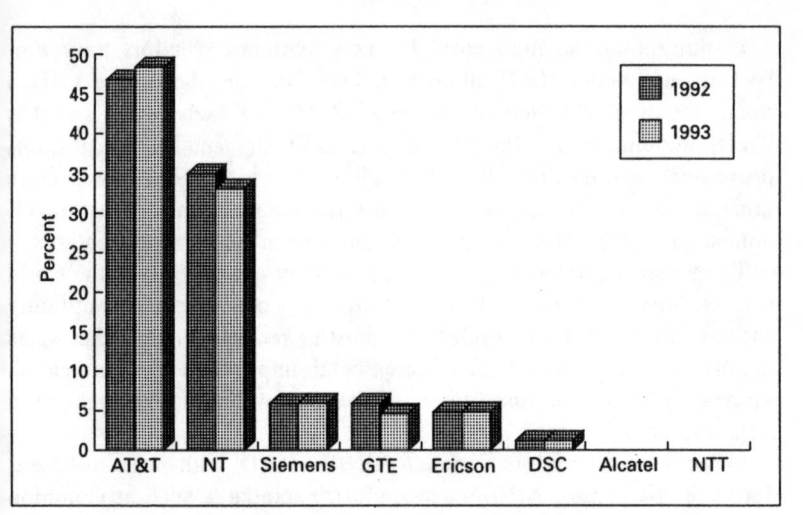

Source: Nortel Daily Information Service, September 1, 1994; available from Northern Business Information, Inc.

Figure 10.1   Top Vendor Market Shares in US Public Switch Market

Telecommunications equipment manufacturers must develop large central office (CO) switches that are extremely expensive to develop and operate. Development costs for a new switch average \$1–\$1.5 billion in a market that is tied-up between eight major players (see Figure 10.1). Rising R&D costs, shrinking government subsidies, and more new suppliers makes for a tight knit group of established companies.

The top switch vendors compete head to head with computer manufacturers as computer and communications technologies merge. Switch manufacturers have forged alliances with major computer software houses to develop switch intelligence. Computer manufacturers such as IBM want to unbundle 'the smarts' from the switch and make it open for competition. The alliance for computer–telephone integration (CTI) formed by computer manufacturers is setting standards for programmable telephones, televisions and switches. For example, CTI member IBM wants to remove the intelligence from telecommunications switches and place it in a separate unit.[2] The separation of software from the switch would allow computer manufacturers to develop the software that would put the smarts into the network. Switch manufacturers collaborate in their own standards-setting alliances to keep computer manufacturers' involvement to a minimum.

In mitigating the high costs for new switches, vendors have embarked on a major R&D alliance making crusade. According to Dan Stanzione of AT&T Network Systems, 8–15% of each switch's cost is R&D, amounting to $100–300 per line. Software and incremental improvements account for 80% of development costs.[3] Not only is there great R&D cost, but the success of a switch can depend on fast development, flexible software upgrades, and enhanced services features.

To recoup development costs, approximately one-seventh of the world market must be captured. To ensure market acceptance and continuing success of a product line, cycle times must be reduced, enhanced services features made available, and incremental improvements regimented. Strategic alliances are used to instill the competitive advantages that a large organization may lack.

Major switch vendors conduct AIN/IN R&D with 'garage-based' software companies. AIN/IN uses industry standards such as Common Channel Signaling #7 (CCS7), Open Network Architecture (ONA) and Integrated Services Digital Network (ISDN) to help independent software developers write applications for vendors' switches. The key for switch manufacturers is to base as much of the product as possible on open standards. The software developer will modify software specifically for each interface of a vendor's switch.

The quickness of getting customer-driven solutions to market (sometimes referred to as *service velocity*) is critically reliant on partnerships. The Baby Bells demand features for their public networks that must be deployed within a calculated window of opportunity. If that window of opportunity is missed, competing carriers may take the market and feature development will have been for naught. This rivalry forces Baby Bells into close partnership with equipment manufacturers. Equipment manufacturers, in turn, forge alliances with software houses that can rapidly develop the software needed to address the market opportunity. The velocity of development depends on positive synergies between companies.

Alliances with small entrepreneurial-driven companies accelerate development and reduce costs. Small companies have the drive, flexibility, adeptness and specialized skills to deliver cost-effective customized solutions. Larger, more mature organizations benefit from alliances that are specifically focused on entrepreneurial projects with rapid turnaround times.

Adding new features to most existing AIN/IN software affects many different parts of the software and so modifications necessitate extensive rewrites. This is a time-consuming and inflexible approach that

accounts for a significant portion of R&D stated above. Coherence with industry standards allows independent software developers to create software that is compatible with any number of compliant switches. Flexible Service Logic (FSL) is the architectural paradigm developed by Northern Telecom's Bell Northern Research and is an industry standard for developing network services. The building block style of FSL allows easy addition and deletion of new features without major re-writes. Since FSL has a stable, well-known interface, software developers can redevelop different features such as call forwarding, caller ID, and voice messaging without disrupting existing services.

Every time a feature is revised, the software must be down-loaded onto the switch and activated. A switch cannot normally be 'rebooted' so the ability to change and add features during live switch operation is difficult. The object-oriented FSL system allows new features to be added without disrupting existing services. New features can be deployed and only that feature which is affected must be 'rebooted.' Since outages are costly in terms of lost service revenue, liability for outages, and detrimental effects on customer satisfaction, they must be avoided if at all possible.

The AIN/IN business is extremely competitive. The life cycle of an application can be as short as 12 months and the window of opportunity half that. Bells respond to market opportunities by partnering with equipment suppliers. Equipment suppliers, in turn, work in close partnership with software developers on high task complexity projects. Suppliers reduce the cost of goods sold through a flexible switch architecture based on industry standards. Innovation and renewal are essential characteristics of a successful supplier's strategy. Only through strategic alliances for standards, service definition and deployment can windows of opportunity be accurately addressed.

10.2.1 Internal Applications Development

The growth in the AIN/IN market has heightened the competition between suppliers. One supplier's strategy has been to create an internal business unit that accelerates time-to-market of new products and services through internal cross-product teams and strategic alliances. The team is responsible for systems integration, product modification, and adjunct development. It delivers quickly and stimulates rapid, low-cost service creation by combining internal and external resources. The equipment supplier is in a partnership with customers who sell AIN/IN services retail.[4]

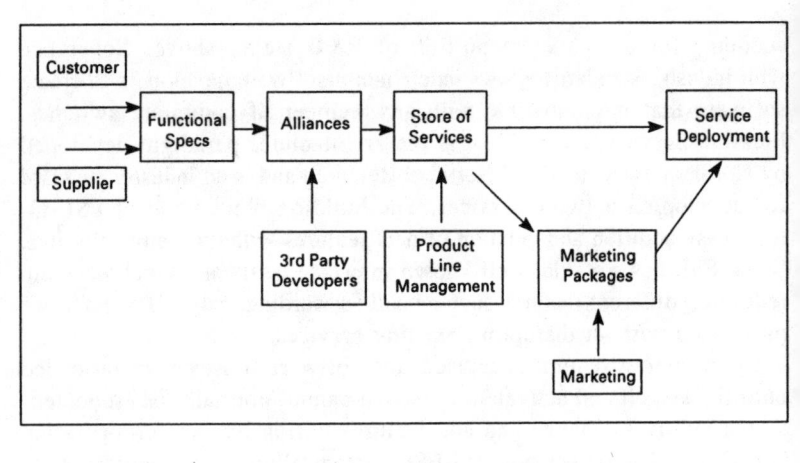

Figure 10.2   A Business Model

From the start, an optimum mix of internal and external development groups is organized in concert with customer requirements. The team uses a demand-driven versus a technology-driven strategy, assigning design teams to work with individual customers and their subscribers. The team is free to choose external partners over internal development teams for any project. Internal groups actually compete on a project-by-project basis with external software companies.

Management fulfills its commitment in alliances by responding to market drivers. If there is any question as to who should do the development, the customer can make the decision. Striking the right balance between internal groups and external alliances can be a difficult management task when the customer has the final say.

Through a business model as shown in Figure 10.2, the customer and the supplier are brought into a commercial partnership. The goal is to create the most effective solution for the customer that is sold in an agreed-upon time-frame. The supplier provides the technology and marketing expertise required to productize customer opportunities. The customer has the best first-hand market knowledge but may need help in defining the functional requirements for the new service. Once the supplier and customer agree on a set of requirements, the supplier seeks third party developers that can rapidly develop services.

An array of software development alliances produces a store of services that can be reused or ported to different systems. The services can be delivered directly to the customer that had contracted development. Competitive advantage through technology push is created if

there is enough synergy with market-pull applications from store of services. Services can be adapted to other markets depending on product line management and supplier–customer initiatives. Marketing packages can be developed which address opportunities for new or altered services from the store. Emphasis on early customer focus assures both the customer and supplier develop accurately defined, customized applications within short delivery times. At least one major sale (to the original contractor) is always assured.

The customer focus requires a brand-new cultural environment that couples the developers directly with the customer. Cultural changes require streamlining the work, simplifying the relationships, and removing the hand-offs. It requires re-educating employees in a new way of thinking about the customer. Increasing competitiveness of suppliers requires complete dedication to the customer, and all suppliers must accept the changes. The major switch suppliers such as AT&T, Alcatel, Nortel and Siemens use alliances to address markets and induce cultural changes.

Northern Telecom's ServiceBuilder Toolkit

Northern Telecom's ServiceBuilder is a pre-made toolkit that helps third parties develop AIN/IN services for Nortel's switches. The toolkit allows alliances to produce results with a minimum starting time. It helps develop new applications as customers define new requirements. ServiceBuilders allows new scenarios to be rapidly developed, deployed, tested, re-developed and delivered.

Baby Bells can justify development of new features by increase in the number of telephone calls connected and increased traffic revenues. For example, in Figure 10.3, 30% of all long distance calls from *A* to *B* are not completed or receive a busy signal; 50% of these calls are never repeated. A 2% increase in the toll completion rate means $100 million a year in additional earnings for the Bells. In the US, a 2% improvement is worth $825 million for the inter-exchange carriers (e.g. AT&T, MCI, Sprint) and $635 million a year for the intra-exchange carriers (Baby Bells). ServiceBuilder can increase the number of services available to connect calls.

The Service Creation Environment (SCE) is a part of ServiceBuilder using Bell Northern Research's FSL (see Figure 10.4). The components of the integrated communications/computing system are: (i) the Intelligent Peripheral (IP), an open platform based on Northern Telecom's Flexible Vocabulary Recognition technology, (ii) the Service Control

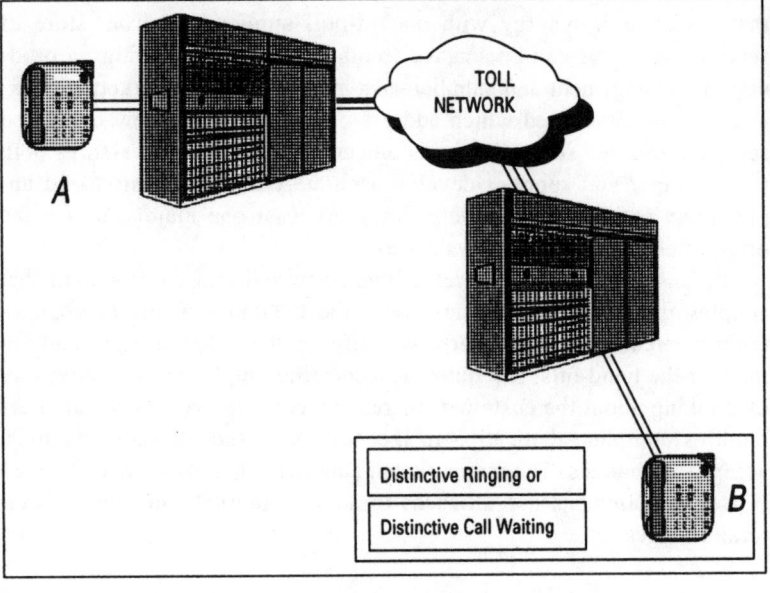

Figure 10.3   Long-Distance Call Completion

Point (SCP), a computing platform built on DMS-100 technology with an open architecture integrated with UNIX-based computers, (iii) the Service Management System (SMS), a suite of UNIX-based management tools and programs for integrating service management functions, and (iv) low-cost terminals for widespread deployment.

Some services that can be developed using the ServiceBuilder system are:

- *Personal Call Management*: End-users may want an intelligent agent to connect with the network. The intelligent call agent acts as an intermediary/distributor. It feeds into a roaming virtual office that can be the recipient's home, office, boat, etc. Faxes, electronic mail, telephone calls, and video can all be routed to the user no matter what the location. The intelligent agent can route all calls or only route high-priority calls for the user's attention. The end user is protected while retaining full access to a range of outgoing communication services.
- *Home Location Register/Visiting Location Register (HLR/VLR)*: HLR/VLR is used by both terrestrial and cellular systems to track billing

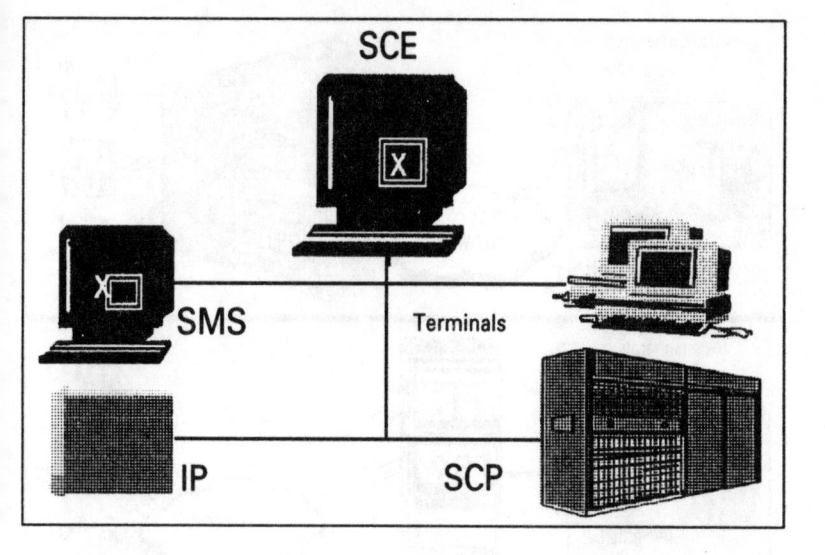

Figure 10.4   ServiceBuilder's Service Creation Environment

of cellular phones on the move. The difficulty is in managing the transition to and from home and visiting territories. Home territory is the area controlled by the service provider which issued the cellular phone number. When the customer leaves home territory, for example from SNET to NYNEX's territory, database synchronization is required for billing. A new communications signal is provided (a procedure called *hand-off*) from NYNEX. Obviously, NYNEX wants to be paid for its cellular services and will eventually reconcile accounts with SNET. Information such as time of entry, time of exit, duration of call(s), services used, number of calls, and time periods is exchanged. Companies abide by a standard format for the exchange of data agreed upon during contractual negotiations. The function of HLR/VLR is to assist service providers in calculating inter-company payments.

- *Automated Call Distribution (ACD), Voice Recognition/Generation (VR/VG)*: Telemarketing and market research use automated call distribution (ACD) and voice recognition/generation (VR/VG). Marketing firms can cover a much greater population if the process is automated, requiring human intervention only after a call is connected. AIN applications such as ACD and VR/VG have created an

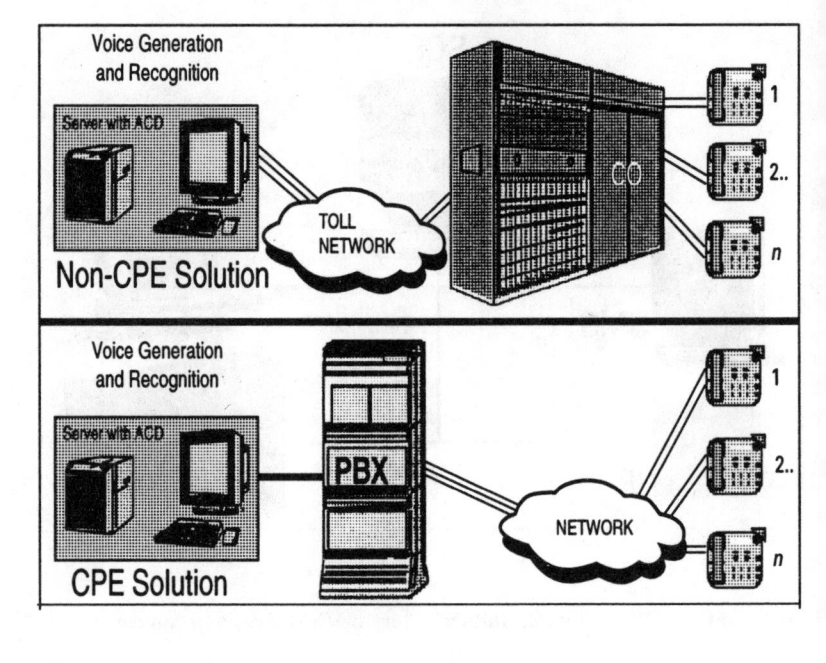

Figure 10.5   Telemarketing using Voice Generation/Recognition

entirely new segment of low-cost competition in market research. The telephone service provider is creating a lower-end market segment that creates new content traffic for services: a perfect example of technology push.

Questions can be pre-recorded and asked over the phone by the voice generation system. Automated call generation is achieved through automatic dialing and voice generation. In other words, the computer both makes the call and talks. The ACD system distributes incoming and outgoing calls according to the availability of lines. The voice recognition system understands the responses to the queries and records answers in a database. Human intervention is only required when the computer cannot understand the calling party's responses.

As shown in Figure 10.5, customers can use a non-CPE solution that places most of the network intelligence on the central office (CO) switch. All AIN/IN ACD and voice recognition/generation applications run on the CO switch. The only hardware that is located on the customer's premises is the Server. The non-CPE solution provides the greatest revenue to the service provider.

Customers using a CPE solution will have both the Server and

the Private Branch Exchange (PBX) located on premises. The CPE solution provides the greatest independence from the service provider and minimizes the cost of toll calls. The customer can create ACD and VR/VG applications independently from the service provider. This may be preferable when specialized needs dictate development independent from the service provider.

In summary, the ServiceBuilder platform is a good paradigm for joint development with strategic alliance partners. It allows both technology- and market-driven applications to be developed in step with customer requirements. Windows of market opportunity can be taken advantage of with flexibility through large developer capacity and even anticipated through the store of services. Having standardized interfaces allows rapid ramp-up using existing libraries of applications. SCE is an ideal paradigm for using strategic partnerships to develop a large base of compatible software. Having applications that cater to and germinate new market segments is key to service providers' strategies. Standard development toolkits allow rapid reaction to market opportunities by maintaining stores of services.

10.3 PRATT & WHITNEY'S AEROSPACE ALLIANCES

Pratt & Whitney is a leading aircraft engine manufacturer that has extensive experience with strategic alliances. In the 1970s, Pratt & Whitney acted as the main contractor to produce jet engines for McDonnell Douglas and Lockheed. Pratt & Whitney summoned available industry partners that had expertise in building jet engine parts. The partners included major engineering firms such as Honeywell and IBM. The exact specification of the engine would only be known after all alliance partners had time to sit down and discuss overall contractual requirements. Generally, each alliance partner knew that the customer wanted a Pratt & Whitney engine with 21 000 pounds of thrust, for example, the JT8D. Pratt & Whitney had to ally, productize, and then deliver these engines.

The 1990s' jet engine production market is highly competitive and requires strategic alliances. Aerospace alliances include International Aero Engines (IAE), Lockheed–McDonnell Douglas, GE–SNECMA, Airbus Industrie, and Boeing–JCAC. IAE is a joint venture comprised of Pratt & Whitney, Rolls Royce, Fiat, MTU, Japan Aero Engines Corporation and Ishikawajima–Harima Heavy Industries.[5]

IAE was set up to produce a new generation of 25 000-pound thrust engines that would make partner firms competitive in the 20 000–30 000-pound thrust jet engine market. The joint venture considerably reduced the financial risk that each firm took in entering this market. Pratt & Whitney was responsible for the core and rear sections of the engine, MTU and Fiat for the low pressure turbine and gearbox, and Rolls Royce and JAEC for the engine's front section. IAE had sole marketing and project management control since marketing control by any partner would be prone to conflicts of interest.

Mainly due to US Defense Department export controls, Pratt & Whitney and Rolls Royce had kept international technology transfer to a minimum. This reduced organizational complexity in technology transfer and empowered partners. Individual alliance partners were encouraged to develop their engine parts independently and rely on blueprints without testing the interfaces. The integration of all components was later fraught with difficulties since integration of the components had not been previously tested. Most of the problems were fixable but Rolls Royce had to accept a major burden in redesigning the engine's compressor. The complete integration of the engine was severely delayed and resulted in lost orders. At that time, the future of the alliance seemed uncertain.

In order to save the engine, Pratt & Whitney assumed overall project control and instituted a strong trust-building programme at IAE. The programme included bimonthly meetings at different member companies' headquarters. At these meetings, it was openly discussed how partners would protect themselves in different situations including violations of the alliance agreement.[6] In 1993, IAE ex-president Robert E. Rosati rejoined the consortium as President to rebuild the trust of Pratt & Whitney and Rolls Royce shareholders. Only through open discussions, role-playing, and executive support did the organizationally complex IAE consortia regroup.

The V2500 programme is now on the upswing after successful delivery of the engine for Airbus Industrie's A320 aircraft and the McDonnell Douglas MD-90 aircraft. IAE is seeking to expand its engine line through Pratt & Whitney's advanced Duct Prop technology in a Super Fan engine. Marketing of the engines has been expanded and potential customers include the 727 re-engining programme and the Airbus Industrie A340. Expansion plans include developing a major alliance with an airframe manufacturer for integrated aircraft production. By reevaluating the alliance and initiating open discussions, IAE was able to spring back and deliver. By rebuilding trust, this alliance was saved.

11 Telecom Equipment Integration at Unisource

Strategic alliances often require equipment from different partner companies to be integrated, a process called *systems integration*. Each partner begins with equipment, account management, help desk support, and service provision capabilities. After an alliance is finalized, equipment and services must be integrated. Escalating problems and establishing responsibility can be difficult across multi-carrier networks.

Systems integration is costly and the long-term cost justification may be based on the longevity of the alliance. Since most strategic alliances result in failure or acquisition, full integration is sensible only as long as each partner accepts a respective financial burden. The extent of integration depends on the investment made and the commitment to the longevity of the alliance.

11.1 THE PARTNERS

Unisource is a rapidly growing telecommunications consortium that has been a popular pan-European alliance in the eyes of most industry watchers. Figure 11.1 illustrates the ownership structure of Unisource. The Swedish, Dutch, and Swiss PTTs, and Telefonica each own 25%. Spain's Telefonica is a relatively new partner and is merging its 'Red Uno' network with Telefonica's 'Unidata' network.

AT&T wants to solidify its relationship with Unisource and may start a new company owned by itself (60%) and Unisource (40%). AT&T would employ 4000–5000 people at the alliance, more than all US carriers have in Europe. The company would provide telecommunications services and global network integration through its WorldPartners programme and WorldWorx products. WorldPartners allows partners to sell seamless services throughout the world.

Unisource and SITA (Société Internationale Telecommunication Aeriennes) have combined their equipment bidding and are tendering for a 1000 node, global ATM network. SITA itself has nodes in 214 countries and recently formed the North American Unispan consortium. Unispan consists of EMI Communications Corp., Integrated Network

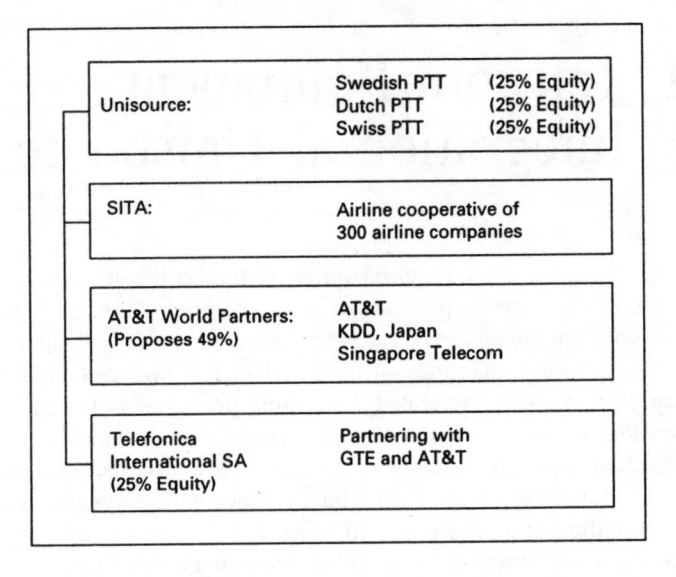

Figure 11.1   The Emerging Global Unisource Consortium

Services Inc., Intermedia Communications of Florida Inc., and Pacnet Inc.[1] SITA's commercial arm, Scitor Ltd., has been integrated back into SITA and offers frame relay service in 57 countries.

11.2   THE EQUIPMENT

As shown in Table 11.1, Unisource, SITA and Telefonica; British Telecom and MCI; and France Telecom, DBP Telekom and Sprint have different types of equipment for X.25, Frame Relay, IP, and VPN services. Integrating the equipment of each alliance partner is complex and costly.

In the past, telephone utilities worked together to integrate equipment according to technical standards. This provided end-to-end functionality for the end-user but services were less complex. In today's environment, integrating across hardware platforms according to standards is slow and non-competitive. According to Goran Forslund, director of operations and development for Unisource,

Manufacturers have purposely made it difficult for their products to interwork with those of other vendors. But that strategy is backfiring now that some of the world's most powerful service providers

Table 11.1   Services and Hardware Platforms of Major Service Providers

Alliance	X.25	Frame Relay	IP	VPN (voice)	ATM
Unisource	Nortel	Stratacom Telecom (13)	Cisco (NA) (13)	Several Vendors (8)	Out to tender
SITA	Nortel (200)	Nortel (40)	Cisco (50)	Nortel (200)*	Out to tender
AT&T World Partners	No offer	Stratacom (3)	No offer	Several vendors (3)	No offer
British Telecom	Tymnet (38)	Stratacom (18)	Out to tender	AT&T (NA)	Trialing
MCI	Tymnet (114)	Wellfleet (NA)	No offer	Ericsson (19)	Trialing in US
France Telecom	Alcatel & Philips/ TRT (17)	Alcatel & Philips/ TRT (17)	Cisco & RCE (17)	Several Vendors (13)	Trialing
DBP Telecom	Nortel & Siemens (1)	Nortel (1)	Siemens/ Alcatel (1)	Trialing	Trialing
Sprint	Alcatel Data Networks (14)	Alcatel Data Networks (14)	Cisco (4)	Nortel (18)	No offer
Telefonica	Nortel	Nortel	Cisco	AT&T, Nortel	Trialing

Notes: *Data only.
NA: Not available.

Source: Schenker, J., 'Alliances Face Integration Headache' (*Communications Week International*, July 18, 1994, 26).

are merging their networks. Up to now, network management has been proprietary. Vendors will either have to gamble everything on one fortune card or cooperate in a new way.

Unisource is using software that is written on top of the hardware for integrating different equipment. This allows hardware to remain the same while advances in software increase the compatibility of different systems. For example, AT&T's Worldworx system is a network-level application that provides seamless connections between competing products.

The Network Management System (NMS) used to monitor equipment was once different for each vendor's equipment. Twenty network management systems on different computers are needed to monitor Unisource's network. But according to SITA's Salama,

> If the [SITA–Unisource] alliance grows stronger and involves equity shares, we will have to migrate to consistent network management.

The NMS systems would be integrated and one workstation could monitor the entire network.

To help alleviate dilemmas before they become issues, Unisource partners are jointly bidding and purchasing. Soon new equipment purchases for the Unisource network will be made only by consensus. According to SITA's Vice President of alliances, Raoul Salama,

> by issuing a joint Request for Proposal [RFP], you ensure compatibility of equipment and you have the advantage of higher buying power.[2]

Although different vendors' equipment will always exist on the network, a more orderly evolution will emerge as partners come to understand the logistics of their decisions.

12 Internal Ventures

The difficult things to remove are the rigid walls between the functions and the constituencies of a company: finance, manufacturing, engineering, sales, management, labor, customers, and suppliers. Each boundary, with its jargon and turf defense and parochial interests, is a speed bump that slows you down, muffles your communications, and makes you less productive and responsive. By getting rid of them and creating real cross-functional teams are orders of difficulty more difficult than vertical de-layering (J. Richard Stonesifer, President and CEO of GE Appliances, commenting on GE's restructuring).[1]

Breaking down the barriers within organizations to form internal ventures has been a key of company turn-arounds in the 1990s. Companies that change hierarchical cultures and promote cross-functional, cross-divisional or cross-whatever collaboration discover huge productivity increases. For example, General Electric changed its corporate culture through 13 years of direction under Jack Welch. Division heads were told to look inwards to other businesses within the GE family and make successful ventures from within. The heads of business units encouraged their employees to look outwards for strategic alliance opportunities. The combination of a strong, productive internal core and the external synergy of alliances radically changed GE's corporate culture, turning the company around. GE's cash flow and profitability is now higher than ever before.

Equipment makers and the Bells have long been compartmentalized because of an affinity to regulation. Telecommunications markets have been heavily regulated, making for a bureaucratic and somewhat regulated corporate culture. Now that telecommunications is moving towards free competition, companies are changing with the environment.

Inducing cultural change requires incentive changes such as promoting team-oriented people with a zeal for working across organizational boundaries. Those who create successful new business ventures hold a key in developing the new culture. Integrating movies and entertainment moguls into a regulated public utility would have seemed unthinkable 10 years ago. Now these persons are developing business opportunities between movies and telephones.

Several case studies of internal ventures are presented below. The

95

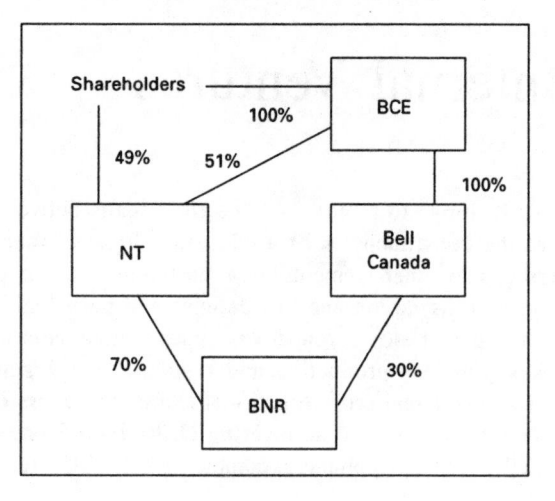

Figure 12.1   Nortel–BCE–Bell Canada–BNR Relationships

first case explores the Nortel–Bell Northern Research–Bell Canada Enterprises relationships and its new corporate culture. Additional case studies focus on internal R&D, marketing and customer service.

12.1   NORTEL–BELL NORTHERN RESEARCH–BELL CANADA ENTERPRISES

Nortel is an incorporation of several companies (see Figure 12.1). As a telecommunications equipment maker, Nortel requires a strong, flexible and responsive R&D operation. Its main R&D operation is Bell Northern Research (BNR), the joint venture between Nortel and Bell Canada. BNR develops products for both Nortel and Bell Canada and obtains its funding through multiple project sponsorships. Bell Canada Enterprises (BCE) influences BNR by controlling both Nortel and Bell Canada. In turn, BNR asserts bargaining power in development decisions through after-sales support commitments. Nortel asserts its bargaining power on internal partners by using more external alliances.

As shown in Figure 12.2, the customer is relied upon to drive the product development process. Individual processes (in this case, business units) responsible for *Strategic Development, Concept to Prototype, Production, Order Fulfillment* and *Inquiry-to-Resolve* have been empowered to move closer to the marketplace. The empowerment re-

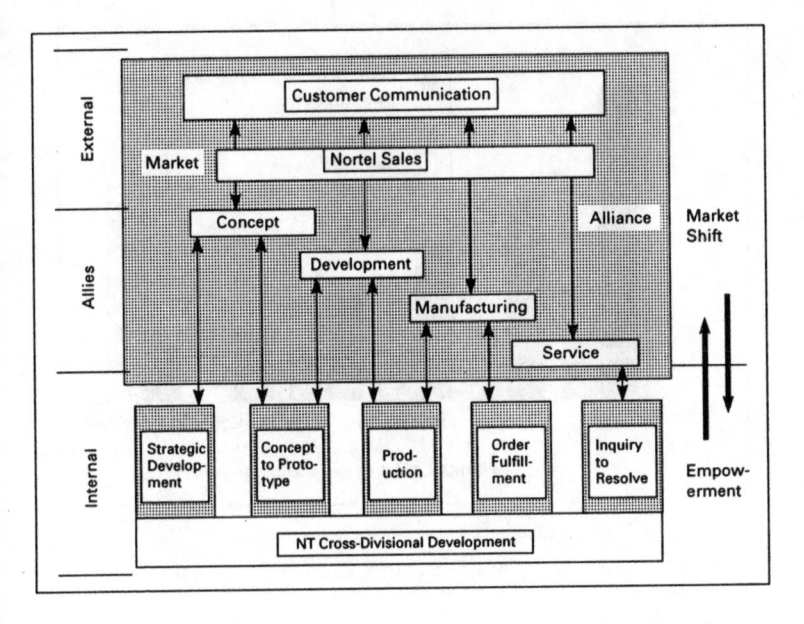

Figure 12.2   Nortel–Partner Product Development

quires individual business units to communicate closely with the customer. At the bottom of the diagram, cross-divisional development is made across individual business units. In the middle section of Figure 12.2, the product life cycle (*Concept, Development, Manufacturing,* and *Service*) is nestled in the market. The organizational lines of company and market have become blurred as a greater reliance on alliances has integrated the market with development. The entire product life cycle requires constant communication with the customer, sales and individual business units.

12.2   NORTEL'S BUSINESSEXPRESS[2]

Nortel launched the internal, cross-divisional alliance, BusinessExpress, to address a market that was new for the corporation. Nortel had traditionally focused on very large national customers that required solutions designed for massive networks. Normally, these customers were national telephone companies, Baby Bells, and Fortune 500 Corporations. Each of Nortel's customers required approximately the same overhead for marketing and sales. Most customers were interested in equipment

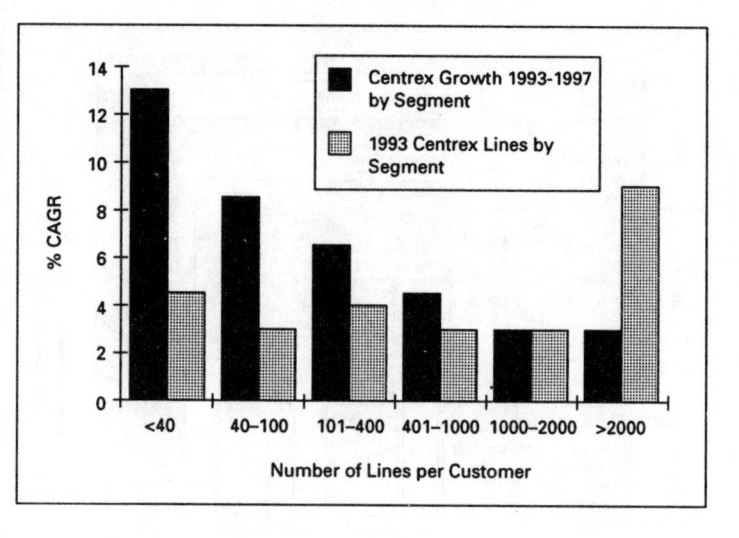

Figure 12.3   Major Centrex Growth Opportunity

designed for reselling services on a public network. Public service providers chose a supplier and continued to buy this supplier's equipment, necessitating relatively little sales effort. Small customers were in another market that was not as critical to Nortel's revenue base.

The need for intelligent small company solutions developed into a strategic market for Nortel. Competitiveness in telecommunications due to the fractionalization of service providers, consolidation of computer and telecommunications technologies, and decentralization of network intelligence forced major telecommunications equipment manufacturers to reevaluate the importance of small customers. Small businesses increasingly asked, 'What business are we in?'. Separate profit-and-loss (P&L) units were formed, business units were sold off, and existing business units re-engineered around a core mission statement. These initiatives led to a leaner, more efficient organization that required a more integrated communications system. In June 1994, Nortel formed the internal alliance, BusinessExpress, for developing and delivering small business solutions.[3]

Figure 12.3 illustrates the growth of the Centrex market for small businesses. Each market segment is broken down in terms of how many lines per customer (often number of employees per customer). In 1993, most <40 businesses did not employ Centrex owing to its high cost and inflexibility of service offerings. The greatest growth from 1997 comes

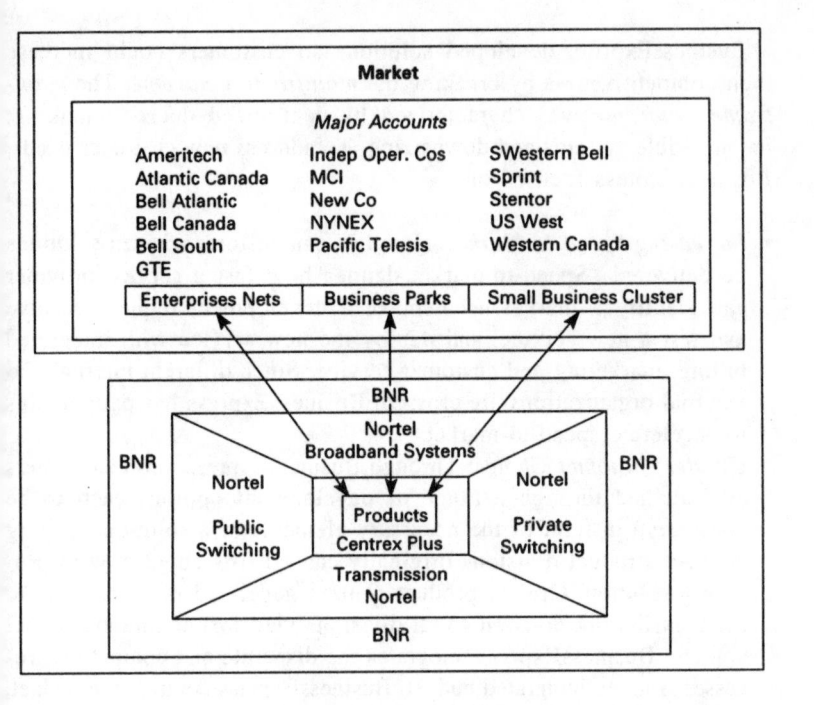

Figure 12.4   BusinessExpress

from the <40 lines per customer category with 13% CAGR (Compound Annual Growth Rate). Small customers found an increasing array of low cost, flexible solutions that met specialized business needs. The >2000 lines category shows the least growth at 3% CAGR but has the largest installed base (3 million lines). Customers with >2000 lines were originally the sole purchasers of central office (CO) switching equipment for customer premises. For the foreseeable future, small businesses represent a strategic market growth opportunity.

As shown in Figure 12.4, internal alliances were formed between Nortel Broadband Systems, Public Switching, Private Switching and Transmission. Each of these divisions supported cross-product teams at BNR. The entire alliance developed products for customers in Major Accounts, Enterprise Networks, Business Parks and Small Business Clusters. The needs of each market were flexibly addressed by BusinessExpress with internal organizations to develop products based on a centralized budget. Intra-corporate collaboration was the basis for the alliance and flexible customer response was the goal.

BusinessExpress developed solutions so customers could increase their competitiveness by breaking the *mainframe syndrome*. The *mainframe syndrome* was characterized by centralized decision making, incompatible systems and downsizing. To address new customer needs, BusinessExpress focused on:

- *Increasing Speed-to-Market*: How fast can customer-driven solutions be delivered? Speed-to-market defines how fast a service provider can identify a market need, make a development request, receive and test a new service, and deploy the new service with integrated billing, marketing and customer service. Since different internal and external organizations are crossed, BusinessExpress has partnerships to accelerate speed-to-market.
- *Greater Customer Choice*: Through BusinessExpress, more customers are satisfied through a range of development options, each to be considered in light of the necessary elements of a solution. Allying between product divisions originally caused rifts about how to provide a solution. Greater product content generated more revenue to the contributing division so all divisions vied for maximum product content. BusinessExpress integrates the disparate and competing processes from an integrated budget. BusinessExpress controls the budget, is results-oriented, and addresses strategic opportunities no matter what organizational boundaries are crossed.
- *More Effective Sales and Marketing*: BusinessExpress has identified the market (see Figure 12.5) and tactics to tackle its potential. Previously, a market of 80 000 lines might have served only one customer. Today, those 80 000 lines might be spread over 800 customers. It is difficult for an established player to simply re-arrange its marketing system and address such a dispersed market. BusinessExpress uses qualified small business partners to work hand-in-hand with customers and deliver solutions through existing channels. Partners are qualified as Nortel sales resellers and linked into a process-oriented supplier/reseller relationship.

12.2.1 BusinessExpress Marketing

The marketing efforts of BusinessExpress focus on (i) engaging resellers to market and sell products and (ii) direct sales. Nortel's direct selling developed a new market for business units within the large corporation. The new marketing effort caters to both intra- and inter-corporate strategic alliances. The alliances require that companies tie themselves in to

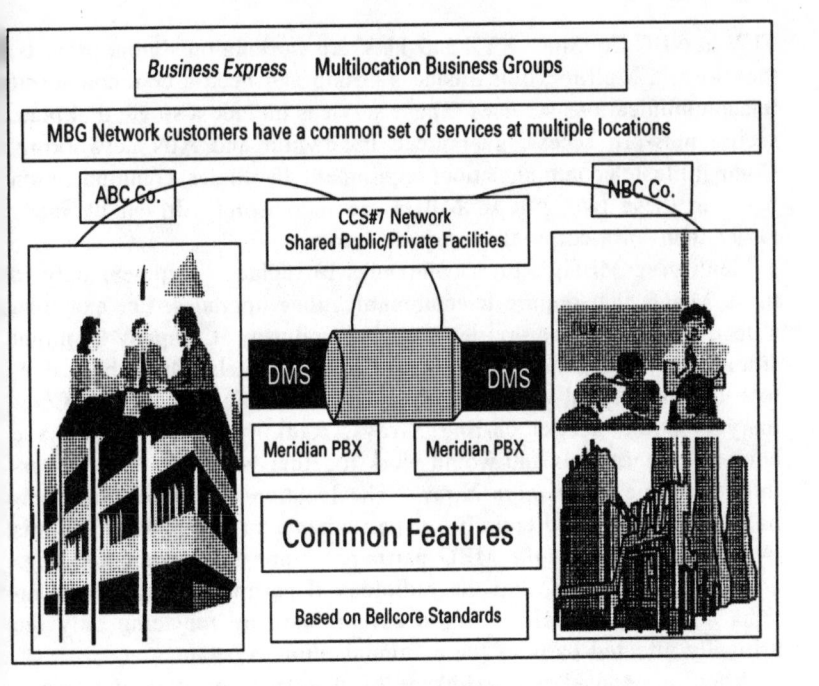

Figure 12.5 Multilocation Business Groups

suppliers, distributors, developers, and customers through integrated voice and data networking.

Multilocation Business Groups (generically referred to as Communities of Interest) are becoming important markets within the multinational corporation. Multilocation Business Group (MBG) is a term that could mean, 'Those people who talk together the most.' It doesn't matter whether they are co-located, whom they work for, or what their role in the business process is. The crux of the MBG determination is, 'Between whom is the most traffic for each telecommunications service?'. If several different companies' systems and locations are crossed, tracking the MBG can be especially difficult. The actual determination of meaningful MBGs is done with traffic analysis tools that assist in the process. Network engineering tools such as those from X-Cell Communications assist in automating this process.

In the following example, the ABC and NBC companies have a strategic alliance requiring close cooperation between the two groups. As shown in Figure 12.5, there is group XYZ at ABC Co. and group

TUV at NBC Co. Since XYZ and TUV are working on similar projects, they form a Multilocation Business Group and need a common set of telecommunications services. These services include a single dial plan, secure network access, guaranteed bandwidth and AIN networking. Compatible telecommunications equipment facilitates communication between these two groups. MBGs are increasingly driven by inter- rather than intra-corporate communications.

Identifying MBGs allows companies to replace equipment only in those MBGs that require telecommunications upgrades. For example, a document storage and retrieval service company (Company Q) might store X-Rays of patients from major area hospitals. Only those doctors in each hospital who have terminals compatible with those at Company Q could access on-line X-rays. Radiology might also have compatible terminals and would work together with a doctor in determining the need for more X-rays. The location of compatible terminals would be based entirely on participants in the process. In this hypothetical process, the MBG participants are the document storage company, the doctor, and the radiology department. Upgrading systems according to MBGs would save money by replacing only the critically affected parts of the communications system.

When one considers interlinkage of all major hospitals, the associated MBG becomes very large. If an experienced specialist in another hospital has access to a compatible terminal, then a better decision can be made. Interlinking communities allows the groups to perform their mission by facilitating outsourced document retrieval and storage. Marketing efforts are assisted by proving the effectiveness of upgrading according to MBGs. Upgrading an entire telecommunications system without regard for MBGs is not only costlier but can cause incompatibilities with existing MBGs.

12.2.2 BusinessExpress Products

Developing solutions for Multilocation Business Groups requires a heavy emphasis on internal ventures within Nortel. Bringing the needs of different users together in the same MBG requires integrating different systems. Customers make their switches communicate and support their MBG needs at the least cost. All features are developed and based on the Bellcore CCS#7 industry standard. Custom AIN/IN applications based on CCS#7 can operate across different hardware platforms.

The BusinessExpress' Centrex system (Meridian 1 PBX) allows businesses to provide a certain amount of switching on customer premises.

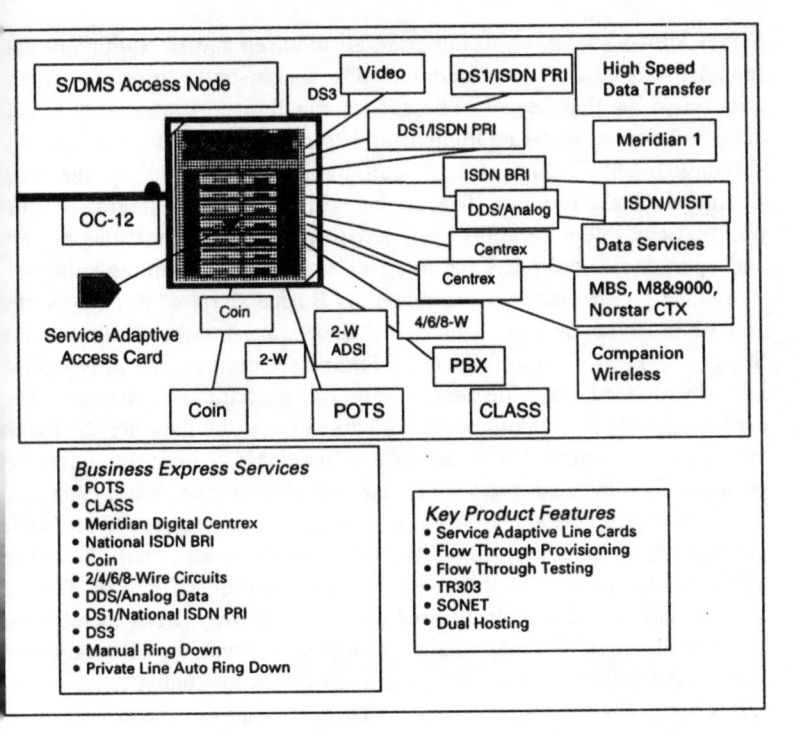

Figure 12.6   Multi-Service BusinessExpress Server

Examples of Centrex benefits include: (i) dialing another employee's extension without needing an outside line, (ii) centralized voice messaging access from anywhere in the network, (iii) call routing between offices on leased-line facilities, (iv) telephone conferencing, and (v) wireless communication. Essentially, a business saves money by avoiding use of the public networks' switching facilities. The cost justification for a Centrex system is better for large businesses with larger phone bills. But small businesses increasingly find Centrex systems justifiable for both cost savings and productivity reasons.

Developing a Centrex system that was capable of integrating systems from different MBGs was a major challenge for BusinessExpress. One of the key products behind the BusinessExpress strategy is the MultiService Server shown in Figure 12.6. This product was developed by an internal venture between the Nortel switching and transmission divisions. Switching integrated their S/DMS Access Node and transmission, their OC-12 FiberWorld TransportNode. The MultiService

Server allows switching to integrate all required access equipment and funnel the bandwidth requirements into a fiber-optic 'pipe' for transmission to another server. The server can transport whatever data it collects from attached equipment and transmit it to other servers. All services listed in Figure 12.6 can be accommodated by the new BusinessExpress product. The server will provide an integrated solution that can integrate almost any existing telecommunications system and upgrade critical parts for more effective MBG communication.

Another product under development by BusinessExpress through Nortel and BNR is the Service Adaptive Access card for the Multi-Service Server. Services such as ISDN, POTS and Centrex can be provisioned and downloaded onto the server without any hardware changes. The card is flexible for accommodating new services as they are deployed throughout an entire MBG. Members of an MBG may not have the power to coordinate an upgrade of their system with other MBG members. Software downloads allow Nortel to download new features to all MBG members simultaneously. Once the new service is activated, the entire MBG should be compatible with the new feature. If a new feature must be developed specifically for one MBG partner, BNR develops it and downloads it directly to the appropriate server. In summary, the Service Adaptive Access Card eliminates hardware changes and accelerates service velocity, improving customer responsiveness.

In summary, BusinessExpress uses internal ventures and strategic alliances to address marketing and product development demands that would not otherwise be possible. Strategic alliance partners provide the manpower to give personalized sales and support to smaller customers. Internal ventures provide the necessary development resources and flexibility to respond to customer demands. Centralized budgeting focuses on product development from beginning to end no matter what internal organizational units are involved. The speed of bringing solutions to market is accelerated through close partnerships between customer, supplier and internal business units.

13 Re-engineering an Alliance: A Customer Service Program

The following case study illustrates the use of re-engineering internal ventures/strategic alliances to greatly improve customer service. The Service Improvement Program (SIP) shows how strategic alliances with customers and developers are a natural part of good customer support.

The Service Improvement Program increases customer satisfaction ratings by engaging the customer as a partner. Through pro-active programs in customer support, customer needs are anticipated and engaged before they become issues. Fully anticipating issues requires working together with the customer in every action affecting customer satisfaction. Some of the important Service Improvement Program goals are shown in Figure 13.1.

13.1 INTRODUCTION TO RE-ENGINEERING

Re-engineering is the process of redesigning business processes according to the goals of the organization. Re-engineering aims to improve a process exponentially and to do it fast. This differs from Continuous Improvement (CI) which is the methodology of trying to improve an existing work process without any fundamental changes. For example, employee surveys and suggestion systems are key components of customer service. But the depth of changes actually made based upon surveys and suggestions is what differentiates re-engineering from continuous improvement. Re-engineering fundamentally changes the work flow and produces leaps in performance. Processes are completely redesigned and streamlined. Redundant, non-value adding procedures are eliminated. Once the process chain has been re-engineered, Continuous Improvement makes small, finely tuned adjustments.

Re-engineering can only succeed with a high-level of executive support. As shown in Figure 13.2, business strategy requires executive support in the form of missions, goals and rules. The re-engineering plan provides

- More substantive response on deployment/development questions
- Better delivery and response times
- Better software quality
- More direct contact with the right persons
- Faster product development times
- Increased value to customer
- Input from customer during development

Figure 13.1   Service Improvement: Program Goals

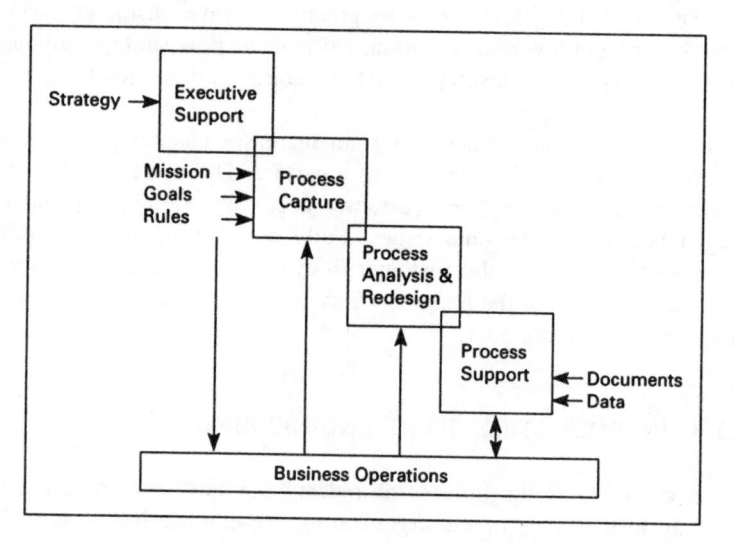

Source: *Product Process Watch*, 1 (London: Enix Ltd., 6).

Figure 13.2   Spectrum of Re-engineering Activity

the tactics required to achieve the Critical Success Factors[1] of the sponsoring executive. Garnering executive support at the highest level is the most important starting point for any re-engineering project.

Communication with operations management is made for important opinions critical to implementation. The team should not drop a re-engineering plan into an executive's lap and expect operations to change based on the plan. The re-engineering diagram is a reflection of arguments to be presented to those who have the power of implementation. The diagrams serve as a guide throughout the implementation process.

High level executives must be given great incentive for re-engineering because:

* Re-engineering may broaden the scope of the process
* Re-engineering costs time of critical operations staff
* Operations must eventually be convinced

Goals and benchmarks of the re-engineering effort are decided upon between the re-engineering team and the executive sponsor. Benchmarks are defined by itemizing the areas needed for improvement. If the goal is 'to improve customer service,' then problem areas from customer surveys should become targets for the re-engineering effort. Benchmarking is performed by measuring future against previous customer survey responses. Benchmarking can also be performed by the executive in measuring how well each re-engineering goal matches Critical Success Factors (CSFs). The executive can monitor how well each CSF is being fulfilled. Once the mission statement, goals and rules are defined, the re-engineering team can begin capturing the process.

13.2 PROCESS CAPTURE AND BUSINESS MODELING

Process capture and business modeling shows the process as it presently exists. Process capture is done by a group that is performing the task being re-engineered. For the following case study, a group is assembled of persons involved in relevant aspects of customer service. The goal is to involve the customer in the product development process so products more closely match customer's needs. The final result is a more satisfied customer.

The power of re-engineering starts with the objective diagnosis of what is presently happening. It is most effective to model 'as is' before modeling 'to be' and allowing the team to diagnose the present state of affairs. The entire process need not necessarily be modeled, rather the important parts that are to be re-engineered should be carefully diagrammed. The goal of re-engineering (to improve customer service, for example) is kept in mind during every stage. The model reflects the Critical Success Factors pertaining to the executive-approved re-engineering mission statement. By maintaining compatibility with the Critical Success Factors, top executive support should continue.

Once the re-engineering team feels that it has achieved a good

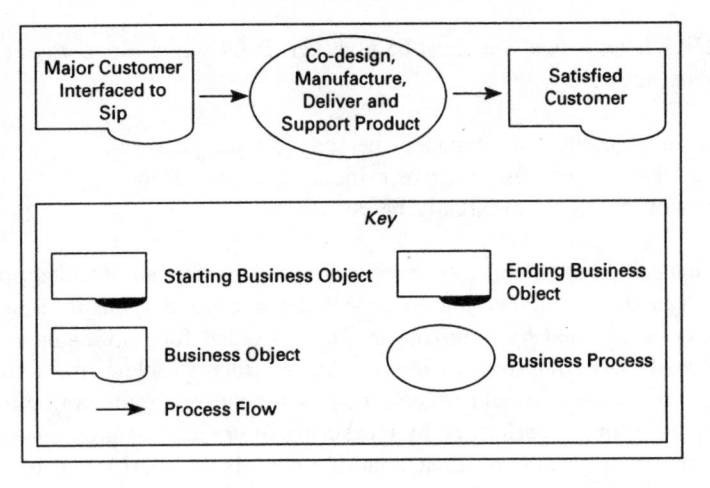

Figure 13.3   Service Improvement Program, Top Level

understanding of where they are, modeling the process as it should be is started. At this stage, a re-engineering tool becomes important. The tool tests different 'to be' scenarios. It helps team members try new interfaces, processes, business objects and support systems. It automatically tracks increasing levels of detail while keeping in sight the whole picture. The most popular re-engineering tools are based on the flow methodology described below. Flow is intuitive for operations teams that are familiar with process content and not re-engineering.

As shown in Figure 13.3, flow charts depict how the work flows. Each flow chart is composed of business objects and process flows. A business object is a finite non-changing object like a report or goal. Each process receives business object inputs, performs a process function and produces the output from the given inputs. Keeping each process function simple, yet effective for the whole flow diagram, is the key to good diagramming. Developing concise and relevant process functions is an art developed through experience. Each process should not be viewed in isolation, but with respect to other processes. The interlinkage of process flow diagrams should achieve a common goal.

Since the flow diagram depicts the chronological order in which processes and business objects flow, it is easy to understand what is happening. The same business object can affect different chronological points in the process. The names of processes and objects should be kept easy to understand even if they are lengthy names. Who performs

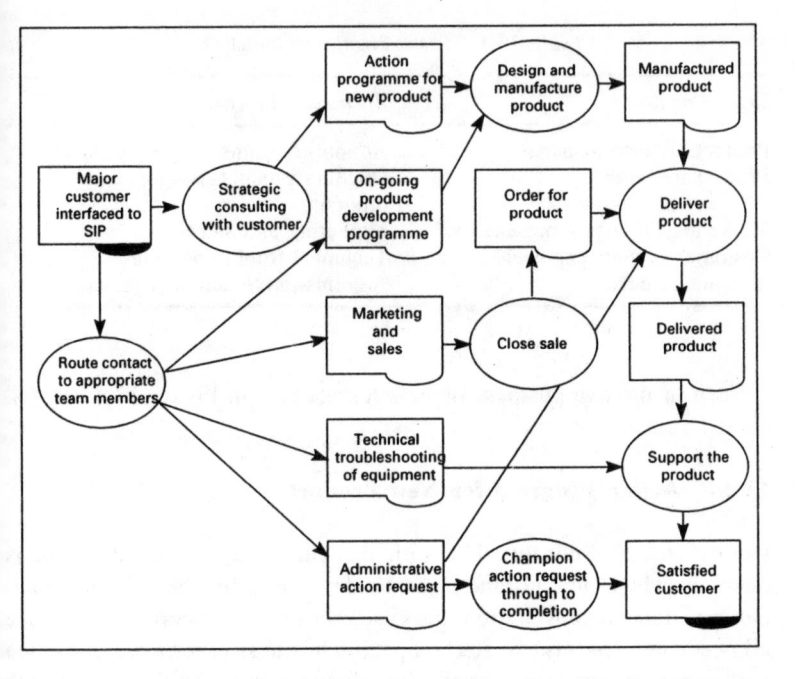

Figure 13.4   SIP: Co-design, Manufacture, Deliver and Support Products

each process is not always shown on the diagram to keep it less cluttered.

As shown in the re-engineering flow chart in Figure 13.3, a customer is interfaced with the Service Improvement Program (SIP) for *Co-Design, Manufacture, Deliver,* and *Support.* The first business object, *Customer Interfaced with SIP,* represents a milestone. The process of *Co-design, Manufacture, Deliver and Support the Product* ultimately leads to a satisfied customer. The final business object is a milestone representing that satisfied customer.

The five employees who form the Service Improvement Program team are assembled to address customers requiring customer satisfaction improvements. Each team member has at least six months to dedicate to the SIP team. Re-engineering programs like SIP provide exponential improvements that are accomplished only by dedicated efforts. An improvement in customer satisfaction ratings is the reward for the re-engineering efforts.

Corresponding with Figure 13.4, team positions and corresponding business objectives are given in Table 13.1.

Table 13.1   Team Positions/Objectives

Team Position	Business Objective
Product alliance manager	Action programs for new products
Product manager	Ongoing product development programs
Marketing or sales representative	Marketing and sales
Customer support engineer	Technical troubleshooting
Account manager	Administrative action requests

Each of the five business objects represented in Figure 13.4 are discussed below.

13.2.1   Action Program for New Product

During strategic consultation with the customer, a joint decision is made on which new products can be developed for the SIP customer. During strategic consultation, the customer has the opportunity to voice all needs and concerns to R&D. Specific business criteria are discussed with the customer. Internal capacity, alliances or a combination of both address customer requirements in product design and specification. If the customer agrees to the requirements of the program, then the Action Program for New Product continues.

The customer always sees the corporation as an entity that delivers new products based on the customer's criteria. All strategic alliances are operationally transparent to the customer while the customer may be informed that the corporation is using an alliance to develop a product. It is the responsibility of the SIP team to relay the ease of 'one-stop shopping' to the customer.

13.2.2   Design and Manufacture

The original process of Design and Manufacture incorporated only two options (see Figure 13.5): *outsourced to strategic alliance partner* and *internal development by single product group*. These two options allowed either (a) outsourcing all R&D or (b) performing all R&D by a single, internal product development group. There was little room for compromise between the two solutions.

As shown in Figure 13.6, more options for product development are available. The product alliance manager can try various means of de-

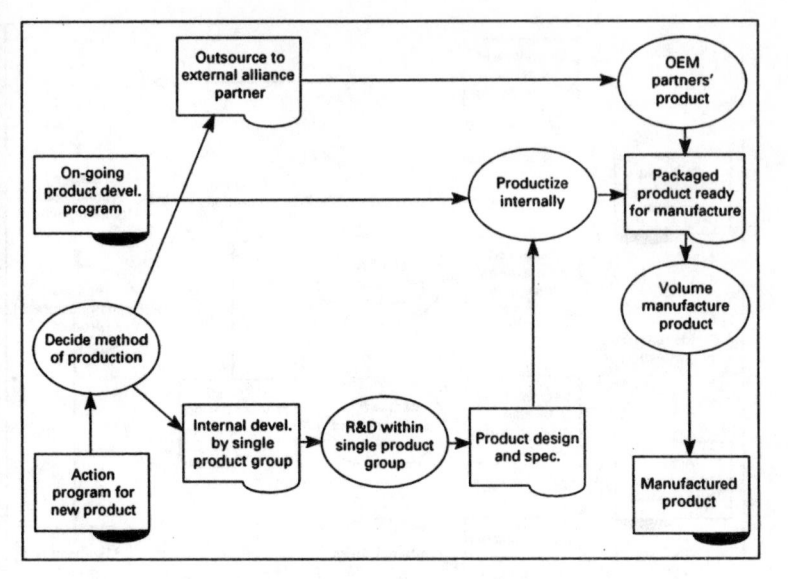

Figure 13.5   Original Design and Manufacture Product

signing and developing the product including the business objects: *outsourced to strategic alliance partner, insourced from strategic alliance partner, internal development by single product group,* and *internal venture to create critical mass.* Each is evaluated by the product alliance manager. There are several forms of development available that range from Original Equipment Manufacturing (OEM) to internal development (see also Table 13.2).

If the critical mass that justifies internal development can be garnered, the sponsoring company receives both the revenue stream and all the R&D capacity. An internal venture to create critical mass can be built through cross-product groups. Alternatively, the required capability can be insourced from a strategic alliance partner and integrated into internal productization. The final business object of process, *Design and Manufacture Product,* is the *Manufactured Product.*

If outsourcing to a strategic alliance partner is chosen, the partner simply acts as an original equipment manufacturer (OEM) and is not involved in R&D. OEMing is the least costly method of production. The OEM product carries the sponsoring corporation's name and support. Although OEMing is least expensive in the short term, it may prove more expensive in the long term. Logistical issues during product

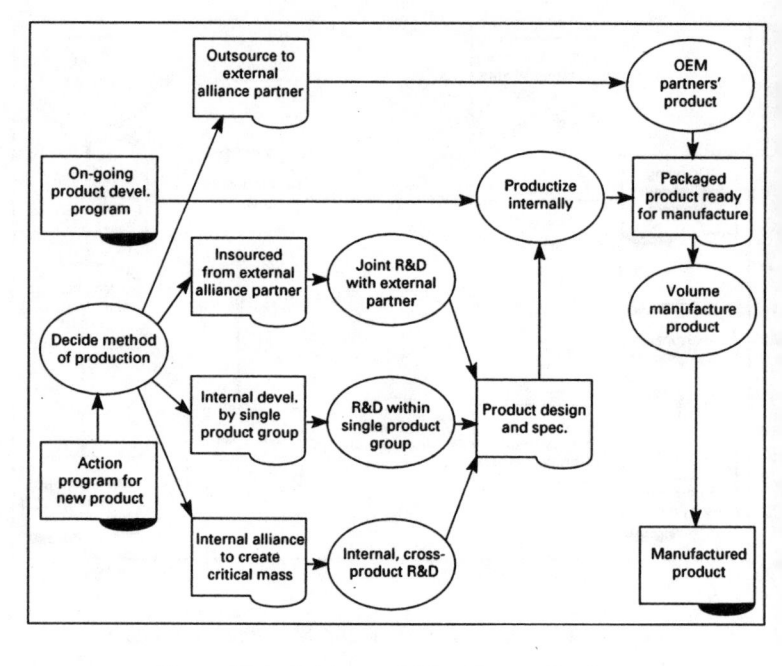

Figure 13.6   Design and Manufacture Product

revisions, new product introductions, and technical support can be troublesome when all product expertise is in a non-affiliated partner. OEM deals must be carefully evaluated based on product complexity, alliance partner's reputation, market need and support requirements.

13.2.3   Ongoing Product Development Program

Once an *Action Program for New Product* is underway, the customer uses the SIP interface: *On-going Product Development Program*. The customer is provided with direct input into product management and contacts are exercised sparingly. The *On-Going Product Development Program* provides the customer with the opportunity to track and maintain a certain amount of product development control. The end-result is a product compatible with all objectives agreed upon during strategic consultation. The customer continually provides input into the product development process.

If an internal venture creates the product, the product alliance manager must join the separate business units together in a process. The product manager puts the customer in direct contact with appropriate

Table 13.2 Product Development Options

New Product Development Method	Major Input
Outsource to Strategic Alliance	Packaging, delivery, possible support
Insource from Strategic Alliance	Technical development from partner; sponsor provides major input during productization and support
Internal Venture to Create Critical Mass	Several internal divisions are encouraged to cooperate and the product is developed with existing expertise
Internal Development by Single Product Group	Sufficient, internal capacity and capability exists to develop and produce a new product

developers as needs dictate. No design changes are made without appropriate programme meetings where the customer addresses issues. Customer issues should be understood well before productization. The product manager has the added responsibility of meeting with the customer and maintaining the alliance.

13.2.4 Productization

As shown in Figure 13.7, the field trial evaluations assure customer input during the *On-going Product Development Program*. From *Product Specifications and Design*, products are manufactured in trial quantity. Productization is performed by the combination of product groups and alliance partners, as discussed above. After the product passes prototype development, field trials are performed. Field trials are performed with the customer sponsoring the research. From the field trial evaluation and meetings of the *On-going Product Development Program*, the product passes field trial testing and can be delivered for sale back to the customer.

13.2.5 Administrative Action Requests

Figure 13.8 shows *Administrative Action Requests* used by the account manager on the SIP team. The account manager champions important

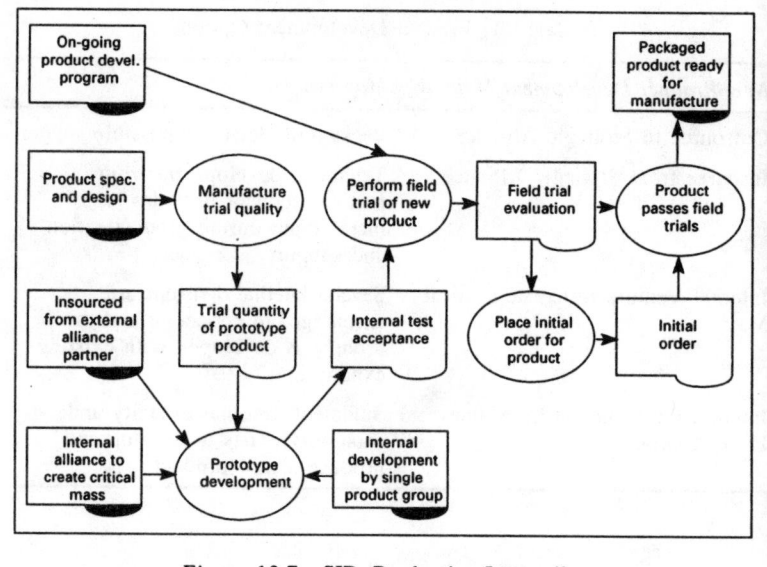

Figure 13.7   SIP: Productize Internally

tasks (defined by the customer) through the required channels. The account manager assures the customer that there will be a timely delivery of the product and expedites delivery through the *order recording, custom clearance,* and *returns processes.* The information system is used to support both order processing and delivery. For maximum effectiveness, the customer orders products directly from the information system.

13.2.6   Technical Troubleshooting

Figure 13.9 shows that the customer interfaces with *Technical Troubleshooting of Product* as part of the SIP team. The customer is educated on the product through participation in the *On-going Product Development Programme.* The corporation continues product value by maintaining a high standard of after-sales support for all products, whether the product is developed internally or through strategic alliances.

Both the customer and the sponsor use an information system to identify issues affecting the product. When the problem is solved, the SIP team member sees that the solution is promptly implemented and delivered. The information system is updated and informs others that a solution has been found. Customer support engineers perform the ongoing field work.

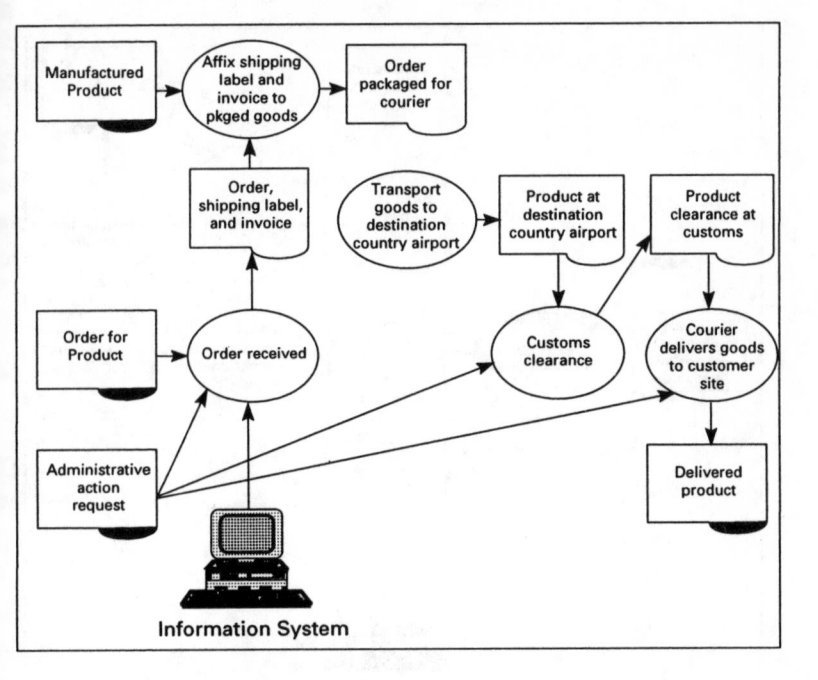

Figure 13.8   Administrative Action Request for Delivery

Ultimately, SIP affects all areas related to Customer Satisfaction. Everything is customer-driven and the SIP team members have addressed customer concerns. The re-engineered SIP processes which use a combination of internal ventures and strategic alliances, ultimately result in a *Satisfied Customer*.

Re-engineering allows the process flows between internal groups and strategic alliances to be mapped. This helps develop consistency, clarity and checkpoints in the partnership. The result is a more efficient and effective partnership that is focused on specific goals.

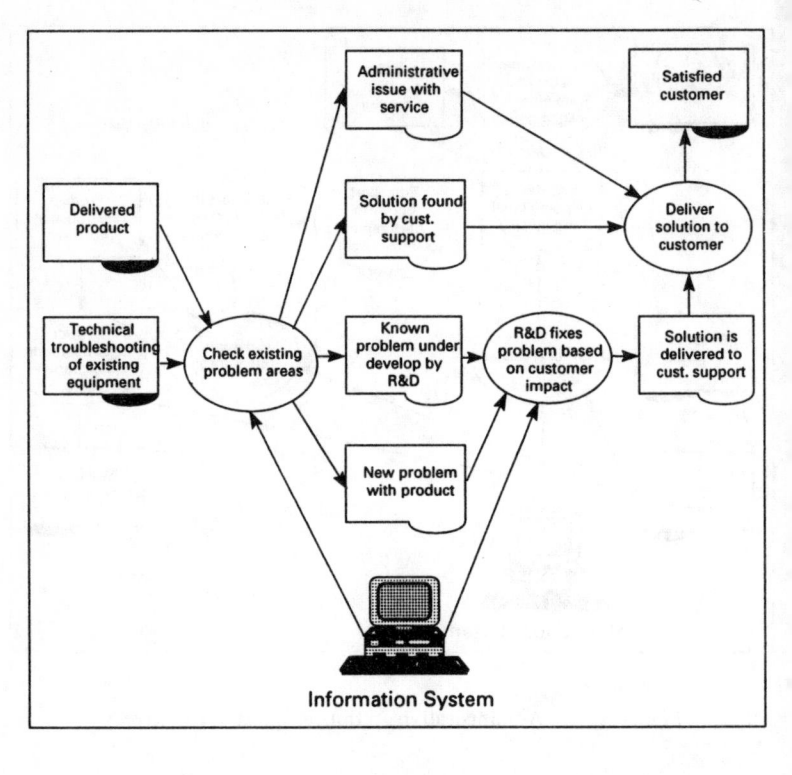

Figure 13.9   Technical Troubleshooting of Existing Equipment

14 Conclusions

The final conclusions of this book are based on a survey of 90 tele-communications, entertainment and communications companies. The results are related to internal ventures and strategic alliance management in telecommunications and multimedia corporations.

The following definitions will help clarify the conclusions:

- *Internal Venture*: an engine for new business development that unleashes core competencies, increases the velocity of their circulation, and builds their size and stock. It requires communication, open-minded thinking and a commitment to working across organizational boundaries.[1]
- *Strategic Alliance*: an inter-corporate relationship that spans vertically or horizontally between two or more firms. Organizationally, it is a joint venture, product swap, licensing arrangement, or strategic alliance. Mergers and acquisitions do not generally count as alliances.

14.1 CONCLUSION: INTERNAL GROUPS ARE COMPETING AGAINST POTENTIAL EXTERNAL PARTNERS

In Figure 14.1, 24% of survey respondents look to strategic partners for meeting specific business objectives. As shown in Figure 14.2, 50% of respondents look internally to find the products, services and support to meet business objectives, 29% of respondents choose whichever partner is best while 21% of respondents find their partners externally.

As shown in Figure 14.3, 84% of all survey respondents would form an alliance even if it meant duplication of an internal group or function. Decision makers are willing to accept duplication, etc. if the external partner can better satisfy a business objective. In summary, internal groups are competing against potential strategic (external) partners.

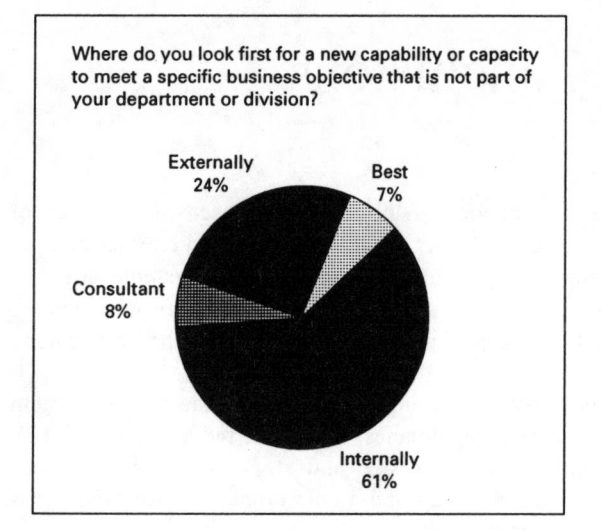

Figure 14.1   Frequencies for 'Look' Question

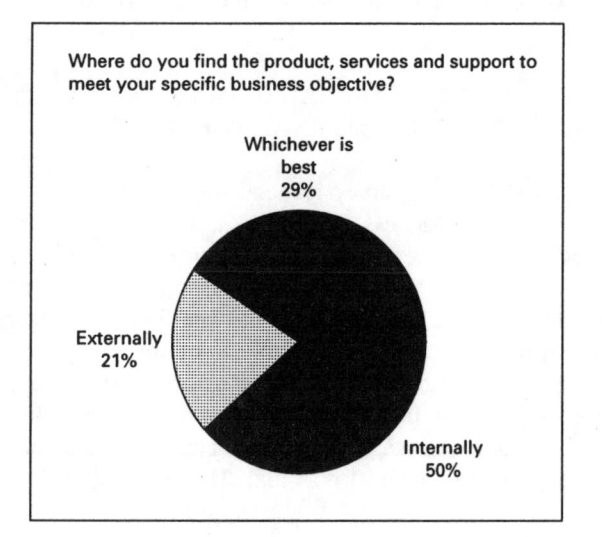

Figure 14.2   Distribution of 'Find' Question

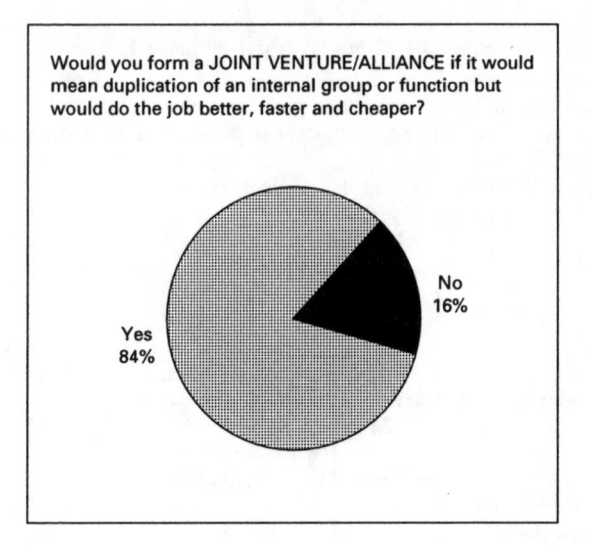

Figure 14.3   Frequencies for 'OK to Duplicate' Question

14.2   CONCLUSION: MANAGEMENT PREFERS INTERNAL VENTURES OVER STRATEGIC ALLIANCES

Table 14.1 shows a cross-tabulation matrix for comparing answers from the questionnaire. The cross-tabulation matrix is used to compare multiple responses on the same questionnaire to see if there are recognizable patterns. Question A is tabulated horizontally and Question B is tabulated vertically.

For example, in the upper left-hand square, 34 respondents both 'looked for alliance partners internally (intra-corp)' and also 'found alliance partners internally (intra-corp)'. The second most popular pattern with 13 cases was 'looked for alliance partner internally' but 'chose the best partner available.' To summarize, respondents seek internal partners and make internal ventures most often.

The cross-tabulation table can be layered according to a third variable. In Table 14.2, questionnaire responses are included only if the respondent chose 'organizational efficiency' as the top motivation in forming alliances. This third, 'layered' variable is seen in the upper left-hand corner of the figure, stating 'controlling for TOP1' and 'TOP1 = Organizational Efficiency.' Only those questionnaires that had chosen

Table 14.1   Look vs. Find Alliance Partner

Question A: Where do you look first for a new capability or capacity for a specific business objective that is not part of your department or division?
Question B: Where do find the product, services, and support to meet you specific business objective?

	Question B:			
Count	Intra-Corp.	Inter-Corp.	Best	Row Total
Intra-corp	34	8	13	55 **61.1**
Consultant **Question A:**	5	1	1	7 7.8
Inter-corp	5	10	7	22 24.4
Best	1		5	6 6.7
Column Total	45 **50.0**	19 21.1	26 28.9	90 100.0

TOP1 = Organizational Efficiency are included in this cross-tabulation matrix (total of 21).

Promoting organizational efficiency is a top management issue that includes specific issues like *time to market, reduction in development time, and more efficient use of resources.* Table 14.2 examines where organization efficiency was chosen as the top motivational factor. It was chosen in a total of 19 cases. Respondents sought internal partners in 13 (68.4%) of the cases but in only 10 (52.6%) of the cases were internal partners found. In only slightly less, 8 (42.1%) cases, the best partner was chosen, whether it was internal or external to the company.

Perhaps organizational alliances are the most controversial. While they may expedite product development, etc., existing internal groups are directly affected. In other words, the motivations for these alliances are not a shortage of internal resources, but rather a need to get some-

Table 14.2   Look vs. Find Alliance Partner with Organizational Efficiency
as Motive

Controlling for.
TOP1 Value = Organizational Efficiency

Question A: Where do you look first for a new capability or
capacity for a specific business objective that is not part of your
department or division?

Question B: Where do find the product, services, and support to
meet your specific business objective?

Count		Question B: Intra-Corp.	Inter-Corp.	Best	Row Total
Intra-corp.		8	1	4	**13** **68.4**
Consultant **Question A:**		1		1	2 10.5
Inter-corp.				1	1 5.3
Best		1		2	3 15.8
Column Total		**10** **52.6**	1 5.3	**8** 42.1	**19** 100.0

thing done faster or more efficiently. As a result, internal groups are
directly displaced through the efforts of more efficient external groups.
It is exactly this type of alliance that causes the greatest resistance
from internal organizations.

14.3   CONCLUSION: CORE COMPETENCIES ARE BEING BUILT AND STRENGTHENED USING ALLIANCES

Core competencies are the essence of what a company is good at. For
example, Corning may be good at Glass and Motorola good at electronics.

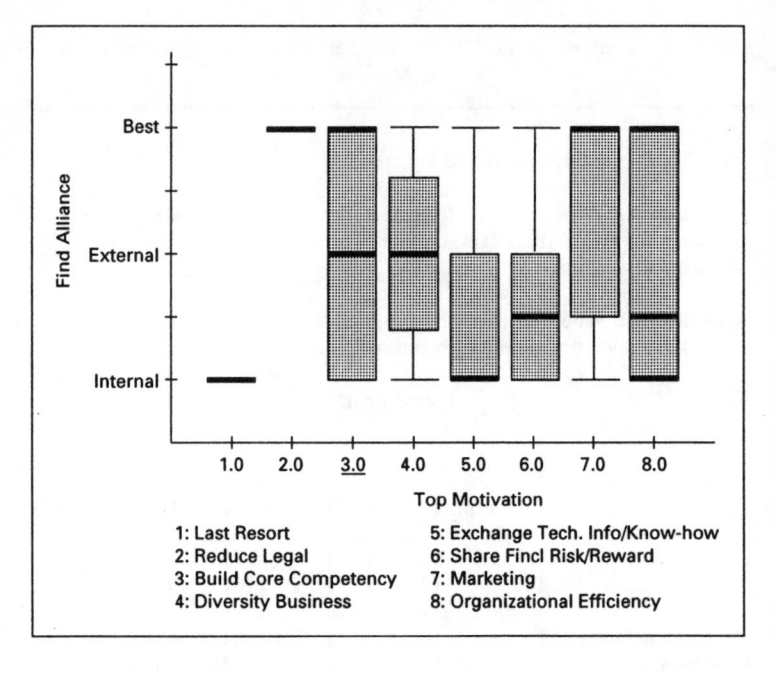

Figure 14.4   Boxplot of Find Alliance vs. Top Motivation

Managers often seek ventures and alliances as a means of building upon existing core competency.

The boxplot shown in Figure 14.4 examines the relationship of strategic objectives to alliance decisions. The boxplot is useful for discovering relationships in data that is cross-correlated. Individual tabulations of data are plotted onto one chart so that the entire data set can be examined. On the Y axis are values that correspond to responses to question 2, i.e. 'Where do you actually find your alliance partner?' On the X axis are the top motivational factors for forming alliances. Each survey respondent had to list three motivational factors and the top factor is correlated here. The values from 1 to 8 correspond to the motivations as shown in Figure 14.1. The thick horizontal line on the graph shows the median, the top and bottom borders of the box show the 25th and 75th percentiles, respectively. 50% of all values fall somewhere within the box.

By examining the Boxplot for Top Motivation 3 (Expand Core Competency) it can be seen that the data is evenly skewed between 'internal' and 'best option.' The survey respondents take the best option

available when expanding core competencies. The even distribution shows that 67% of respondents will choose external or best partner and only 33% of respondents will choose internal partner.

Additional information from the boxplot shows (i) those that use alliances to diversify business (4) tend toward strategic alliances, (ii) those that use alliances to exchange technical info (5) and to share financial risk/reward (6) tend toward internal ventures and (iii) those that use alliances for marketing purposes (7) tend toward strategic alliances.

Sufficient flexibility and communications are key in corporations sharing core competencies in inter-corporate alliances. Managers must respond flexibly to changes in a competitive situation. According to the survey, 79% of companies did have enough intra-corporate. communication with top management to ensure flexibility and funding of joint ventures/alliances. 100% of those managers who used alliances to build core competency had enough communication with top management to ensure flexibility of funding.

In summary, core competencies are being built through strategic (inter-corporate) or best (intra-corporate) alliance partners. The main concern is the vulnerability of companies that use strategic alliances. While the internal venture would be more protective of core competencies, all respondents using alliances to expand core competencies had 'enough communications with management to ensure flexibility of funding.' This might assure a swift buyout of the partner in case the situation became threatened due to lack of control.

14.4 CONCLUSION: THERE IS MORE COMMUNICATION WITHIN THE CORPORATION AND COMMUNICATION IS IMPORTANT FOR STRATEGIC ALLIANCES

Table 14.3 shows that 68 (76%) of all companies with sufficient intra-corporate communication for flexibility also have, or are planning an alliance. This compares with just 9 (10%) of companies that do not have enough intra-corporate communication and have, or are planning an alliance.

The data shows that intra-corporate communication is critical to forming alliances. Since there are more strategic alliances than ever before, it is assumed that there is more communication than ever before. What causes what cannot be directly determined from the data set.

Table 14.3   Sufficient Intra-corporate Communication

Question A: Is there enough communication with top management to ensure flexibility and funding of joint ventures/alliances?

Question B: Have you entered into, or are you considering entering into a joint venture/alliances with another organization for a specific business objective?

Count		**Question B:**				Row Total
		YES	I	NO	I	
Question A: YES	I	68	I	11	I	79
	I		I		I	87.8
NO	I	9	I	2	I	11
	I		I	12.2	I	
Column Total		77		13		90
		85.6		14.4		100.0

14.5   CONCLUSION: ALLIANCES ARE MORE OPERATIONAL THAN STRATEGIC

The top motivations for forming alliances are listed in Figure 1.1 in Chapter 1. The most popular reason, 'share of financial risk/rewards' is an operational objective that is not necessarily strategic. The second most popular category, 'exchange technical info/know-how' can be strategic if the alliance partner has critical knowledge. If the knowledge that the partner shares is critical to developing a new product or service then it is strategic. In most cases, however, the exchange of technical info/know-how is done to save money, reduce development time or increase R&D capacity. According to Ohmae, development costs have become a fixed cost that is nothing more than an entry fee.[2] Reduction of fixed costs is not really a strategic objective. And the third most popular category, 'speed to market' is clearly operational.

Strategic alliances do not appear to be as strategic as is commonly understood. As shown above, the most popular motivations for alliances are not strategic and it can be assumed that strategy is not the primary motivation for alliances. Strategic alliances are just an extension of

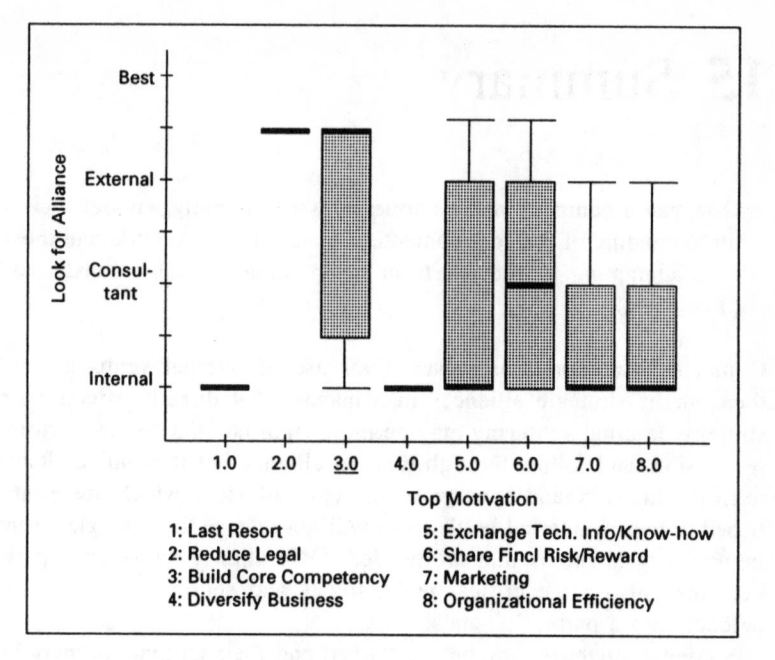

Figure 14.5   Boxplot of Look for Alliance vs. Top Motivation

internal corporate abilities to meet strategic objectives. They are a means of stretching the corporation so that overall objectives can be met.

14.6   CONCLUSION: ALLIANCES ARE MADE WITH MORE LUCK AND CHANCE THAN PLANNING

Figure 14.2 explores where managers look first for alliance partners. Top Motivation = 3 on the Y axis represents the motivation to expand core competency. Figure 14.2 shows that managers tend towards a consultant or external partner in finding new sources of core competency. Managers may also look at other strategic alliances in their industry to determine how to expand their own core competency. For example, in telecommunications, much of the industry and its make-up are discovered by examining other alliances.

The observation of alliances is part of forming strategy. It is difficult to plan each alliance since bargaining and luck often determine an alliance partner. Managers choose the best partner possible, and that may mean changing plans accordingly.

15 Summary

> How can a company make partnerships intelligently without a clear understanding of the core competencies it is trying to build and those it is attempting to prevent from being unintentionally transferred? (Yves Doz).[1]

Competitive corporations master their use of internal venturing and then pursue strategic alliances in a manner that directly affects core strategy. Internal venturing may be more rigorous in terms of start-up, persuasion, and follow-through than an alliance but it promotes long-term productivity and synergies. Strategic alliances which are established to bypass internal bottlenecks will not receive the synergies from internal organizations that are needed. Overreliance on external partners may also place critical technologies and sources of core competence into a partner's hands.

Strategic alliances may be short lived and their termination may be viewed favorably within the firm. In fact, the firm's internal organization may react and create its own competencies in competition with the alliance. After an alliance fails, those managers who extricate the firm from the alliance might be viewed as heroes. Later after the internal organization has a chance to fill the void, the alliance may be viewed favorably as having been a catalyst.

To serve the demands of strategic alliances, internal organizations are empowered to collaborate internally. For example, a customer–supplier partnership puts strains on the supplier to work across company boundaries in fulfilling customers' one-stop shopping demands. Borderless programmes and budgetary incentives are in place so the supplier has authority to respond to customer demands. Internal corporate barriers are broken down and budgets correspond with strategic processes. When employees master their use of internal, cross-product, cross-divisional teams, responding to alliance partners' demands with maximum effectiveness is possible.

The internal venture is a winning idea, especially if employees can convince management that they can outperform strategic alliance partners. The organization is evolving itself to meet the demands that were once met only through external partnerships. Most employees favor internal allying since jobs are being spared and new attempts (often

failed) at outsourcing are not being made. Outsourcing always seems riddled with problems and employees may associate strategic alliances with outsourcing. Even more worrisome to employees is the nature of the outsourcing projects, for example, highly task complex projects such as software design, integrated circuit (IC) design, systems integration, and project management. As Peter Killing[2] has noted, intercorporate alliances are not easily managed for task complex projects. Employees will ask, 'if the old form of outsourcing didn't work, how can it possibly work in completing more complex tasks?'. The corporate culture will never accept the outsourcing idea since it serves always to eliminate the existing organization. Internal venturing is the evolution of an organization seeking survival.

Strategic alliances cannot be used to patch holes in the synergistic corporate web; they must be used with planned proficiency. The administration can assume its long-known niche, i.e. keeping track of relationships. The administration is empowered by being aware of expectations from relationships. Empowerment requires divulging corporate strategy to empowered employees for full understanding. Many means exist for communicating this information, for example, electronic mail, the internet, cellular telephony, and electronic personal digital assistants (PDAs). Managers should assure themselves that employees have the right mix of information critical to set goals. The mix of information should include intra-corporate as well as external, market information. With this information, employees are empowered to decide if the best relationships are internal or external.

Consensus-building is the offensive tactic to the free flow of information. Managers recognize that information is becoming more and more available to interested persons. If strategic information is being communicated, then better, more informed, and more successful business decisions can be made with the right empowerment. Consensus building with the help of corporate steering committees helps to make better decisions. Internal versus external alliances decisions should be based on a complex set of strategic and cost factors. According to Michael Porter,[3] the firm creates competitive advantage through lower cost and differentiation. These two forces should drive all consenses on alliance-making.

Finding the best partner possible is also key to successful alliance making. Database systems exist which can assist deal makers in finding the best partners possible. For example, The *Information Industry Deal Making Directory*[4] is a compilation of 200 company responses to questionnaires about partnering. The Directory aims at 'mergers,

acquisitions, and joint ventures that are paving the Information Superhighway.' Also available is *Telecommunications Report's* Telecom Transaction Database that provides coverage of all major telecom mergers, acquisitions and alliances. Most companies exhibit a dislike of computerized measures, but it is better to use them than form a mismatched alliance.

The implementers of alliances should be involved in initial decision making processes. All literature points to greater success of acquisitions and alliances by keeping operations involved in negotiations with alliance partners. The delegated persons should attend negotiations and keep track of commitments so that they are later implemented. Corporate strategy expert, Yves Doz, has recognized the importance of following through with commitments made during negotiations. The conclusion of negotiations does not mean back to business as usual. Lots of work on implementation must be developed and completed. Better understanding of information that is communicated makes for more successful strategic achievements.

There are few remaining cash cows, especially in telecommunications, that cannot focus on better budgeting. Simply being aware that internal ventures play a greater role has resounding and positive consequences for operations. Strategic budgets can focus on promoting internal, cross-product groups that develop synergies both within and with outside partners. Budgets for gathering and building databases of internal, company-wide information can be developed. Budgets for training employees on programmes to make the corporation borderless can be developed. New means of budgeting should focus on a process from beginning to end, no matter how many organizational borders are crossed. External alliances that were once patches for weak corporate areas can now be more accurately incorporated into corporate budgeting. Budgeting is important for seeing through ventures and alliances and starting real organizational changes.

The result of strategic alliances on the culture of the firm can be that cultures change towards a market-orientation. Employees can be brought into war game scenarios that educate employees on their firm's relative competitiveness. At one company, employees fill in the blanks on budgets during company meetings. Discussions ensue where variations from plan are found. Strategic alliances are only accepted if they clearly have a cost saving and beneficial effect on the firm. When the firm can save money through an alliance, employees must justify why this should not happen. Promoting a better interface with the external environment requires a culture change that eschews the not-invented-

here syndrome and other stodgy corporate mentalities. Corporate cultures should be intimately in tune with how they fit into the external environment.

Finally, corporate policy at the sponsoring corporation has recognized that while alliances and partnerships are of strategic importance to the organization, they must be steered. Often organizations that are not parties to a strategic alliance agreement are later affected by the agreement. In order that strategic objectives as a whole are maintained, a strong steering committee should be founded. The steering committee is formed of executives or delegates who have an overall picture of strategic direction. The steering committee considers all major partnerships and evaluates relationships to internal organizations.

In summary, many companies, especially those in telecommunications and multimedia, are creating an entirely new way of business. Developing the required synergies needed to compete requires a combination of internal ventures and strategic alliances. How management develops organizations and alliances is a critical determinant of competitiveness.

Appendix 1: 1984 Cable Act, Section 533

The Communications Policy Act of 1984 47 U.S.C. @ 533(b).

(a) It shall be unlawful for any person to be a cable operator if such person, directly or through 1 or more affiliates, owns or controls the licensee of a television broadcast station and the predicted grade B contour of such a station covers any portion of the community served by such operator's cable system.

(b)(1) It shall be unlawful for any common carrier, subject in whole or in part to subchapter II of this chapter, to provide video programming directly to subscribers in its telephone service area, either directly or indirectly through an affiliate owned by, operated by, controlled by, or under some common control with the common carrier.

(b)(2) It shall be unlawful for any common carrier, subject in whole or in part to subchapter II of this chapter, to provide channels of communication or pole line conduit space, or other rental arrangements, to any entity which is directly or indirectly owned by, operated by, controlled by, or under common control with such a common carrier, if such facilities or arrangements are to be used for, or in connection with, the provision of video programming directly to subscribers in the telephone service area of the common carrier.

(b)(3) This subsection shall not apply to any common carrier to the extent that such carrier provides telephone exchange service in any rural area (as defined by the Commission.

(b)(4) In those areas where the provision of video programming directly to subscribers through a cable system demonstrably could not exist except through a cable system owned by, operated by, controlled by, or affiliated with the common carrier involved, or upon other showing of good cause, the Commission may, on petition for waiver, waive the applicability of paragraphs (1) and (2) of this subsection. Any such waiver shall be made in accordance with section 63.56 of title 47, Code of Federal Regulations (as in effect September 20, 1984) and shall be granted by the Commission upon a finding that the issuance of such a waiver is justified by the particular circumstances demonstrated by the petitioner, taking into account the policy of this subsection.

(c) The Commission may prescribe rules with respect to the ownership or control of cable systems by persons who own or control other media of mass communications which serves the same community served by a cable system.

(d) Any State or franchising authority may not prohibit the ownership or control of a cable system by any person because of such person's ownership or control of any media of mass communication or other media interests.

(e)(1) Subject to paragraph (2), a State or franchising authority may hold any ownership interest in any cable system.

(e)(2) Any State or franchising authority shall not exercise any editorial control regarding the content of any cable service on a cable system in which

such governmental entity holds ownership interest (other than programming on any channel designated for educational or governmental use), unless such control is exercised through an entity separate from the franchising authority.

(f) This section shall not apply to prohibit any combination of any interests held by any person on July 1, 1984, to the extent of the interests so held of such a date, if the holding of such interests was not inconsistent with any applicable Federal or State law or regulation in effect on that date.

(g) For purposes of this section, the term 'media of mass communications' shall have the meaning given such term under section 309(i)(3)(C)(i) of this Act.

Appendix 2: Bellcore Customers and Areas of Collaboration

Bellcore Customer	Area of Collaboration	Effective Date of Agreement
ADC Telecommunications	provisions limiting antitrust	
Amati, Palo Alto, CA	ADSL	Mar. 25, 1993
ANV	exchange and access services	Apr. 1, 1990
Apple Computer	ATM	Mar. 10, 1992
AT&T	audio and video teleconferences	Jul. 1, 1989
AT&T	high speed access services	Jul. 15, 1989
AT&T	SONET/ATM self-healing ring	Apr. 7, 1994
AT&T	surface emitting lasers	Jul. 1, 1989
AT&T	theories and technologies	Jun. 12, 1991
AT&T	video dialtone	Dec. 3, 1992
Avantek	high speed integrated circuits	May 10, 1985
Bell Canada	ISDN, CCS, AIN	May 20, 1992
BNR Europe Limited	open, distributed computing	Dec. 8, 1992
BNR, Ottawa	provisions limiting antitrust	May 1, 1989
British Telecommunications	open, distributed computing	Dec. 8, 1993
British Telecommunications	telecommunications	Sept. 18, 1991
Chisso, Chiyoda-Ku, Japan	electron beams resist	Apr. 11, 1990
Citicorp Intl Communications	directory services	Oct. 1, 1992
Columbia University	optical network technology	Sept. 2, 1992
Conductus	superconductivity	Jul. 1, 1989
CSELT, Torino, Italy	telecommunications concepts	Jul. 18, 1990
DEC	PCS devices	Nov. 18, 1992
DEC International	open, distributed computing	Dec. 8, 1993
Ericsson Cables	fiber reliability	Nov. 15, 1992
France Telecom	open, distributed computing	Dec. 8, 1993
France Telecom	semiconductor laser reliability	Apr. 28, 1992
Fujitsu	network architecture	Oct. 30, 1991
Furukawa	multi-quantum well lasers	Oct. 30, 1989
GCA	video compression	Aug. 1, 1991
Graphics Communications, Japan	low-bit rate video codecs	Sept. 1, 1988
Hewlett-Packard	wireless access communic. sys.	Jul. 12, 1993
HHI, Berlin, Germany	provisions limiting antitrust	
Hitachi	optical transmission	Sept. 30, 1985
Honeywell	gallium arsenide ICs	Feb. 6, 1985
Hughes Aircraft	optical network technology	Sept. 2, 1992
IBM	broadband X-mission & switch.	Jun. 21, 1993
ICL	open, distributed computing	Dec. 8, 1993
IIT, Santa Clara, CA	video, multimedia communic.	May 13, 1993
Italtel Societa Italiana	ATM and networking protocol	Mar. 10, 1994
ITRI, Hsinchu, Taiwan	digital video and transmission	Jan. 3, 1990

Korea Telecom	algorithms for net demand estim	Aug. 26, 1992
Landis & Gyr		Oct. 21, 1988
Lasertron	strained-layer, quantum lasers	Jan. 6, 1992
Marconi Instruments	open, distributed computing	Dec. 8, 1993
Metro Traffic	personal traffic info services	June 15, 1992
Motorola	thin film fuel cells	Dec. 18, 1992
MSC	semiconductors	May 7, 1987
NEC	superconductor film	Nov. 8, 1990
NHK, Tokyo, Japan	HDTV	Apr. 1, 1988
Nortel Federal Systems	optical network technology	Sept. 2, 1992
Northern Telecom Inc.	HDTV	Jul. 27, 1989
NTT	exchange and access services	Mar. 12, 1990
Open Connexion Pty	open, distributed computing	Dec. 8, 1993
PairGrain	ADSL	Jun. 24, 1991
Penney Company	multimedia dbases, home shop	Dec. 17, 1993
Phillips	screen-based telephone	Sept. 17, 1992
Picture Tel	videoconferencing	Apr. 11, 1989
Pirelli	optical amplifiers	Jan. 19, 1990
Plessey	emitter-coupled logic	May 1, 1988
Prism	video compression	Aug. 1, 1991
PTT Research, Netherlands	experimental HW and SW	May 18, 1992
Racal Data Communications	end-to-end digital connectivity	May 10, 1985
RAM Mobile Data	PCS, two-way messaging	Dec. 3, 1992
Reliance	ADSL	Sept. 27, 1991
Rockwell	high speed semiconductor	Sept. 17, 1991
Rockwell International	optical network technology	Sept. 2, 1992
Rockwell International	SONET/ATM self-healing ring	Ap. 7, 1994
Samsung	object-oriented programming	Apr. 6, 1989
Sarnoff	ADSL and Motion Pictures	Jun. 21, 1993
Siemens	broadband and applications	Dec. 1, 1989
Southwestern Bell Techn.	SONET/ATM self-healing ring	Apr. 7. 1994
Sprint	AIN/IN, Fiber in the loop	Feb. 15, 1993
SUMC, Westwood, KS	understanding telecom.	Jan. 1, 1993
Sumitomo Electric	semiconductor materials	Jan. 20, 1988
Sun Microsystems	ATM	Apr. 12, 1991
Supercomputer Systems	computing	Apr. 11, 1989
Symbolics	animation software	Aug. 30, 1990
Taiwan, RoC	ADSL	Mar. 24, 1993
Tektronix	SONET/ATM self-healing ring	Apr. 7, 1994
Telettra, Milan, Italy	video transmission	Jul. 25, 1988
Telia (Sweden)	access services	Jun. 21, 1993
Texas Instruments	high speed copper X-mission	Jun. 3, 1993
Toshiba	ATM and access services	Nov. 14, 1989
Toshiba	exchange access services	Mar. 24, 1992
TranSwitch	SONET internetworking	Oct. 17, 1991
TRL, Horsholm, Denmark	broadband telecommunications	May 1, 1990
TRL, Horsholm, Denmark	optical communications	May 1, 1989
United Technologies	optical network technology	Sept. 2, 1992
Valhalla Corp.	mathematical models for optical	Jan. 7, 1992
Video Telecom	videoconferencing	Apr. 11, 1989
Vitesse	Gallium Arsenide, ICs	June 16, 1987
VLSI	CMOS VLSI for wireless PCS	Apr. 7, 1993
Washington University	SONET/ATM self-healing ring	Apr. 7, 1994
Wiltel, Inc.	ATM/SONET video networking	Dec. 10, 1993
Xerox	ATM	Aug. 13, 1991

Notes and References

1 Introduction

1. Rosabeth Moss Kanter, *When Giants Learn to Dance: Mastering the Challenge of Strategy, Management, and Careers in the 1990's* (New York: Simon & Schuster, 1989), 115.
2. Peter F. Cowhey and Jonathan D. Aronson, *Managing the World Economy* (New York: Council on Foreign Relations Press, 1993), 68.
3. *Communications Outlook 1993* (New York: Organization for Economic Cooperation and Development, 1993), 11.
4. *Communications Outlook, 1993* 11.
5. Roger J. Kashlak, 'Core Business Regulation and Dual Diversification Patterns in the Telecommunications Industry,' *Strategic Management Journal*, 15 (October 1994): 606.

2 Telephone and Cable Television: The Main Drivers

1. *Business Communications Review*, November 1994.
2. *Communications Daily*, September 26, 1994.
3. 21 F.C.C. 2d 307 (1970).
4. Ibid.
5. 47 U.S.C. @ 224 (1988).
6. 'FCC Policy on Cable Ownership,' A Staff Report, FCC Office of Plans and Policy, November 1991.
7. 47 U.S.C. @ 521 (1982 ed. Supp. IV).
8. 830 F. Supp. 909 (1993).
9. 7 FCC Rcd. 5781, 5847 (1992).
10. 7 FCC Rcd., 5847.
11. Senate Rep. No. 92, 102d Cong., 1st Sess. 18 (1991).
12. Ibid.
13. 830 F. Supp. 909 (1993).
14. Ibid.
15. 472 U.S. 675, 689 (1985).
16. *Communications International*, August 1994.
17. Cablevision Systems Corp., *10-K Report*, 1994.
18, 673 F. Supp. 598 (1987).
19. 282 U.S. App. D.C. 347, 569 (1983).
20. 673 F. Supp. 587 (1987).
21. 900 F. 2d 283, (1990).
22. 993 F. 2d 1572 (1993).
23. *Communications Daily*, 28 November 1994.
24. 'Nothing has Changed to Justify Vacating 1982 Antitrust Consent Decree,' *Telecommunications Reports*, November 21, 1994, 6.

3 US West's Full Service Network

1. Neil Knight, Interview by author, July 26, 1984, Notes from Multimedia Communications Group, US West, Engelwood, CO.
2. 'Interactive Network Milestones,' *USWest Today*, July 7, 1994, 1.
3. 'The Interactive Bazaar Opens,' *Economist*, 332 August 20, 1994, 49.
4. Mark Robichaux, 'Entertainment + Technology (A Special Report): Where the Money Is; the Players: Big Money, Big Ideas, Big Egos: Here are the People and Companies to Watch,' *Wall Street Journal*, March 21, 1994, Sec. R, 16.
5. Out-of-region metropolitan areas include Akron, Canton, Youngtown, Albany, Austin, Bakersfield, Birmingham, Charlotte, Cincinnati, Columbus, Greensboro, Honolulu, Houston, Indianapolis, Kansas City, Lakeland, Melbourne, Memphis, Milwaukee, New York, Orlando, Raleigh/Durham, San Diego, Shreveport, Tampa.
6. Dennis, Yablonsky, 'The US West/Carnegie Group Strategic Alliance,' *Planning Review*, September–October 1990, 18.
7. 'US West's Cable TV Plans in Atlanta Position it for Phone Service There,' *Telecommunications Reports*, July 18, 1994, 19, 32.

4 AT&T's Alliances

1. Jack B. Grubman, 'Clinton on the Wire,' *Institutional Investor*, 27, (July 1993), S31–S32.
2. John Keller, 'AT&T Allies,' *Wall Street Journal*, December 3, 1983, Sec. B, 4.
3. The local loop refers to the telephone wire that connects the curbside telephone wire with the home.
4. 'Robert Allen's Wireless Message,' *Industry Week*, February 15, 1993.
5. Richard L. Hudson, Technology: 'European Companies Speed Shift to Phone Competition,' *Wall Street Journal*, June 24, 1994, Sec. B, 4.
6. Stephen Booth, 'Inside Bell Labs,' *Popular Mechanics*, 171, August 1994, 47.
7. Michael Noll, Professor at University of California San Diego, quoted in Martin Fransman, 'AT&T, BT and NTT,' *Telecommunications Policy*, May–June 1994, 298.

5 Multimedia Alliances

1. Richard Turner and Bart Ziegler, 'Disney to Form Video Venture with Baby Bells; Plan Involves Programming for Southwestern Bell, Ameritech, Bellsouth,' *Wall Street Journal*, August 9, 1994, Sec. A, 3.
2. Timothy L. O'Brien, 'Enterprise: Small Software Companies Link Up with the Big Guns; Multimedia Partnerships are Shaping Content, Design and Marketing,' *Wall Street Journal*, August 5, 1994, Sec. B, 2.
3. Ibid., 2.
4. Ibid., 2.
5. Monta Kerr, 'General Magic Software Pulls Wireless Applications Out of its Magic Cap,' *Computing Canada*, 20, February, 2, 1994, 47, 50.

6. 'General Magic Alliance Includes AT&T, Apple, Motorola,' *Telecommunications Reports*, February 5, 1993, 24–25.
7. 'Multimedia Abracadabra,' *Economist*, February 5, 1994, 67–68.
8. *International Herald Tribune*, October 1–2, 1994.
9. Larry Armstrong, 'Look Who's in the Slow Lane,' *Business Week* March 28, 1994, 28–29.
10. James Daly, 'Apple PowerPC Takes on Intel,' *Computerworld*, December 27, 1993–January 3, 1994, 65, 69.
11. Bradley Johnson, 'PowerPC to Change Computer Battlefield, *Advertising Age*, November 15, 1993, S-1, S-12.
12. Rick Tetzeli, 'Videogames: Serious Fury,' *Fortune*, December 27, 1993, 110–116.
13. Betsy Sharkey, 'Recasting Hollywood,' *Brandweek*, 35, March 28, 1994, 24–29.
14. Joan E. Rigdon, 'Technology: Alliance to Link Big Databases and Notes Users,' *Wall Street Journal*, September 26, 1994, Sec. B, 1.
15. Ibid., 1.
16. 'Lotus Forms Partnership With Intel,' *New York Times*, August 10, 1994, Sec. D, 4.

6 The German Market

1. *Communications Week International*, January 16, 1995, 3.
2. Greg Steinmetz, 'Germany's Proposal to Deregulate Telecommunications is Unveiled,' *Wall Street Journal*, March 28, 1995, Sec. 3, 23.
3. Silvia Ascarelli, 'International: Goldman is Chosen as Top Foreign Bank in Privatization of Deutsche Telekom,' *Wall Street Journal*, November 28, 1994 Sec. A, 14.
4. 'Helping US Telecom Exporters,' *Journal of Commerce*, August 15, 1994, 6A.
5. 'DBP Telekom Slashes US Accounting Rate 43%,' *Telecommunications Reports*, July 11, 1994, 38.
6. Steinmetz, 'Germany's Proposal,' 1.
7. 'FCC Approves BT Investment in MCI,' *Telecommunications Reports*, July 18, 1994, 16.
8. John Blau, 'German Group to Team with AT&T,' *Communications Week International*, February 6, 1995, 1.
9. 'C&W Joins VEBA in Strategic European Alliance,' *Telecommunications Reports*, January 30, 1995, 15.
10. Richard L. Hudson and Audrey Choi, 'International: Deutsche Telekom's Monopoly Status Weighs Heavily on Privatization Plan,' *Wall Street Journal*, November 17, 1994, Sec. A, 20.
11. *Financial Times*, September 22, 1994, 15.
12. 'Interexchange Carriers Oppose Ameritech's Plea,' *Telecommunications Reports*, January 16, 1995, 24.

7 Wireless Communications

1. John J. Keller, 'TRW, Teleglobe Set $2.5 Billion Project for Satellite and Wireless Phone System,' *Wall Street Journal*, November 15, 1994, A2.
2. Carnevale, Mary Lu, 'AT&T, Rivals Face off in Cellular Wards,' *Wall Street Journal*, August 19, 1993, Sec. B, 1 (E).
3. Barbara N. Berkman, 'Sagging Profits Spark Identity Crisis at Nokia,' *Electronic Business*, March 4, 1991, 58.
4. Fleming Meeks, 'Watch Out, Motorola,' *Forbes*, September 12, 1994, 192.
5. Patrick Harverson, 'Hearing an Explosion on the Grapevine,' *Financial Times*, August 22, 1994, 13.
6. Kevin G. Hall, 'Telecom Firms See Fertile Market for Wireless Services in Mexico,' *Journal of Commerce*, October 7, 1994, sec. A, 5.
7. Rahul Sharma, 'Sri Lanka a New Boom Market for Cellular Phones,' September 7, 1994, *Reuters, Ltd.* (Online); available from Reuter News File.
8. Teo Poh Kang, 'Singapore Telecom Set for Battle of the Bells,' *Nikkei Weekly*, September 26, 1994, 32.
9. Andrew Adonis, 'Mobiles Overtake Fixed Phones,' *Financial Times*, August 30, 1994, 5.
10. 'Dance of the Cellular Elephants: Grab a Partner,' *International Herald Tribune*, September 16, 1994, 14.
11. *Communications Daily*, January 5, 1995.

8 Nortel – Ameritech Service Improvement Program

1. Jerry Aiken, interview by author, July 21, 1994, Notes from Vice President's Office, Northern Telecom, Schaumberg, IL.
2. Jordan Lewis, 'Using Alliances to Build Market Power,' *Planning Review*, September–October 1990, 5.
3. New lines from Northern Telecom at Ameritech equaled 350,000 in 1991; 1.2m in 1992, 1.8m in 1993; 1.4m in 1994; 1.0m in 1995. The number of total lines is actually greater than 4 million because of base lines already being installed at the time of the 1991 Ameritech tender.
4. 'Ameritech Earnings,' *Chicago Tribune*, July 21, 1994, 21.

9 R&D Consortia

1. Mary Lu Carnevale, 'Technology & Health: FCC Advances Iridium Project For Satellites,' *Wall Street Journal*, October 17, 1994, Sec. B, 7.
2. Naik Gautam, 'Telecommunications (A Special Report): The Bottom Line; The Next Generation: Beyond Ardis, Beyond Ram, Beyond Cellular, There Are PCs And Satellite Networks,' *Wall Street Journal*, February 11, 1994, Sec. R, 22.
3. John J. Keller, 'TRW Teleglobe Set $2.5 Billion Project For Satellite And Wireless Phone System,' *Wall Street Journal*, November 15, 1994, Sec. A, 2.

4. Keller, Sec. A, 2.
5. Since the merger of McCaw Cellular into AT&T, McCaw's partnerships fold into AT&T's control.
6. Peter Coy, 'Bellcore to its Owners: Don't Hang Up,' *Business Week*, December 13, 1993, 108–110.
7. Smith, Emily and Coy, Peter, 'Pumping up the Baby Bells' R&D Arm,' *Science and Technology*, August 5, 1991, 68–69.
8. *Communications International*, March 1994.
9. Formed in 1990, composed of senior executives of Bells with the mission of improving the cost effectiveness and productivity of Bellcore.
10. Bruce Hoadlev, Paul Katz, and Amir Sadrian, 'Improving the Utility of the Bellcore Consortium,' *Interface*, 23, January–February 1993, 36.

10 Joint Development Alliances

1. Telecommunications Report (Boston: Bain & Company, 1994), 2.
2. Robin Mansell, *The New Telecommunications* (London: Sage Publications, 1993), 174.
3. J.A. Hausman and E. Kohlberg, *The Future Evolution of the Central Office Switch Industry* (Boston, MA: Harvard Business School Press, 1989).
4. Traditionally, copyrighting gave intellectual property rights to the author of the software (one party only).
5. Lynn Krieger Mytelka *Strategic Partnerships: States, Firms and International Competition* (Rutherford, NJ: Farleigh Dickinson Press, 1991), 89.
6. Michael F. Wolff, 'Building Trust in Alliances,' *Research-Technology Management*, 37, May–June 1994; 12–15.

11 Telecom Equipment Integration at Unisource

1. 'SITA Extends Data Reach,' *CommunicationsWeek International*, September 12, 1994, 3.
2. 'Global ATM Network,' *CommunicationsWeek International*, July 18, 1994, 33.

12 Internal Ventures

1. Richard J. Stonesifer, 'The Boundaryless Company,' The Conference Board, 1993.
2. Paul Brant, interview by the author, August 5, 1994, Notes, Northern Telecom, Research Triangle Park, North Carolina.
3. Mark Dill, 'S/DMS Business Express for Small Business,' (Nashville: Northern Telecom News Release, June 28, 1994).

13 Re-engineering an Alliance: A Customer Service Programme

1. Jack Rockart, Director of the MIT Center for Information Systems Research originally defined CSFs to be benchmarked by Management Information Systems (MISs). Critical Success Factors (CSFs) are the key objectives

which each executive must carry out to achieve overall corporate strategy and fulfill fiduciary responsibility. Each CSF may be general and each executive is limited to achieving approximately 10 CSFs for the year. See John F. Rockart and Christine V. Bullen, 'A Primer on Critical Success Factors' (Cambridge, MA: Center for Information Systems Research, Sloan School of Management, 1991), 64.

14 Conclusions

1. See C.K. Prahalad and Gary Hamel, 'The Core Competence of the Corporation,' *Harvard Business Review*, 3, May–June 1990, 87.
2. Kenichi Ohmae, *Triad Power* (New York: Free Press, 1985).

15 Summary

1. See also C.K. Prahalad and Gary Hamel, 'The Core Competence of the Corporation,' *Harvard Business Review*, 3, May–June 1990, 87, 89.
2. Peter Killing 'Understanding Alliances: The Role of Task and Organizational Complexity,' in *Cooperative Strategies*, eds. Farok Contractor and Peter Lorange (Lexington, MA: Lexington Books, 1988), 57.
3. Competit Advantage, 13.
4. *The Information Deal Making Directory* (Boston: BRP Publications, Inc., 1994).

Bibliography

Abernathy, H.L. and Utterback, James M., 'Patterns of Industrial Evolution,' *Technology Review*, 80 (June–July, 1978), 40–47.

Aiken, Jerry, interview by author, July 21, 1994, Notes from Vice President's Office, Northern Telecom, Schaumberg, IL.

Andrews, Edmund L., 'The New Minimalists,' *Venture*, 11 (January 1989): 37–39.

Badaracco, Joseph L. Jr., *The Knowledge Link* (Boston: Harvard Business School Press, 1991), 12.

Barabba, Vincent P. and Zaltman, Gerald, *Hearing the Voice of the Market* (Cambridge: Harvard Business School Press, 1991).

Bartlett, C.A., 'Multinational Structural Change: Evolution versus Reorganization,' in *The Management of Headquarters–Subsidiary Relationships in Multinational Corporations* (Aldershot: Gower, 1981).

Bartlett, Christopher A. and Ghoshal, Sumantra, *Transnational Management: Text, Cases, and Readings in Cross-border Management* (Homewood, IL: Irwin, 1992).

Bartlett, C., Doz, Y. and Hedlund, G., *Managing the Global Firm* (New York, London: Routledge, 1990).

Bleeke, Joel and Ernst, David, *Collaborating to Compete* (New York: Wiley, 1993).

Bloedon, Robert V. and Stokes, Deborah R., 'Making University–Industry Collaborative Resarch Succeed,' *Research-Technology Management*, 37 (March–April 1994): 44–48.

Borys, Bryan and Jemison, David B., 'Hybrid Arrangements as Strategic Alliances,' *Academy of Management Review*, 14 (April 1989): 234–249.

Boudette, Neal E., 'The Nineties: Network to Dismantle Old Structures,' *Industry Week* 238, January 16, 1989, 27–31.

Brant, Paul, interview by the author August 5, 1994, Notes, Northern Telecom, Research Triangle Park, North Carolina.

Casson, Mark, *Internalization Theory and Beyond* (Reading: University of Reading, 1990);

Casson, Mark and Buckley, Peter F., 'A Theory of Cooperation in International Business,' in *Cooperative Strategies*, eds. Farok Contractor and Peter Lorange (Lexington, MA: Lexington Books, 1988), 31–54.

Chandler, A.D. Jr., *Strategy and Structure* (Boston: MIT Press, 1962).

Coase, Ronald Henry, Williamson, Oliver E. and Winter, Sidney G., *The Nature of the Firm* (New York: Oxford University Press, 1991).

Contractor, Farok and Lorange, Peter, 'Why Should Firms Cooperate? The Strategy and Economics Basis for Cooperative Ventures,' in *Managing the Global Firm*, eds. Yves Doz, Ghoshal Bartlett and Gunnar Hedlund (London: Routledge, 1990), 487–498.

Cowhey, Peter F. and Aronson, Jonathan D., *Managing the World Economy* (New York: Council on Foreign Relations Press, 1993), 232.

Cox, Glenn A., 'Reclaiming America's Birthright,' *Executive Speeches*, 9 (August–September 1994), 14–17.

David, Byron L., 'How Internal Venture Groups Innovate,' *Research-Technology Management*, 37 (March–April 1994), 38.

Davidow, William H. and Malone, Michael S., *The Virtual Corporation: Structuring and Revitalizing the Corporation for the 21st Century* (New York: HarperCollins, 1992), 8.

Dent, H.S. Jr., 'Corporation of the Future,' *Small Business Reports 15*, 1990, 55–63.

Dill, Mark, 'S/DMS Business Express for Small Business' (Nashville: Northern Telecom News Release, June 28, 1994).

Doz, Yves, interview with SNET Corporation, video satellite feed, 'How to Create and Manage a Strategic Alliance' (New Haven, CT: SNET, August 22, 1994).

Doz, Y., Prahalad, C.K. and Hamel, Gary, 'Strategic Partnerships: Success or Surrender,' presented at AIB–EIBA Meeting (1986).

Doz, Yvez, Prahalad, C.K. and Hamel, Gary, 'Control, Change and Flexibility: The Dilemma of Transnational Collaboration,' in *Managing the Global Firm*, eds. Christopher Bartlett and Yvez Doz (London: Routledge, 1990), 117–143.

Dunning, J.H., *Explaining International Production* (London: Unwin Hyman), 1988.

Galbraith, J.R. and Nathanson, D.A., *Strategy Implementation: The Role of Structure and Processes* (Minnesota: West Publishing Co., 1978).

Ghemawat, Pankaj, *Commitment: The Dynamics of Strategy* (New York: Free Press, 1991), 16.

Gilfillan, Solum C., *The Sociology of Invention* (Cambridge: MIT Press), 1935.

Gilroy, Michael Bernard, *Networking in the Multinational Enterprise, The Importance of Strategic Alliances* (Columbia, South Carolina: University of South Carolina Press, 1993).

'Global ATM Network,' *Communications Week International*, July 18, 1994, 33.

Hakan Hakansson, *Industrial Technological Development* (London: Croom Helm, 1987), 3.

Hammer, Michael and Champy, James, *Re-engineering the Corporation: A Manifesto for Business Revolution* (London: Nicholas Brealey Publishing, 1993).

Harrigan, K.R., *Managing for Joint Venture Success* (Lexington, MA: Lexington Books, 1986).

Harrigan, K.R., 'Strategic Alliances and Partner Assmetries,' in *Cooperative Strategies*, eds. Farok Contractor and Peter Lorange (Lexington, MA: Lexington Books, 1988), 205–226.

Hausman, J.A. and Kohlberg, E., *The Future Evolution of the Central Office Switch Industry* (Boston, MA: Harvard Business School Press, 1989).

Hedberg, B.L.T., Nystron, P.C. and Starbuck, W.H., 'Camping on Seesaws: Prescriptions for a Self-designing Organization,' *Administrative Science Quarterly*, 21 (1976).

Hedlund, Gunnar and Rolander, Dag, 'Action in Heterarchies: New Approaches

to Managing the MNC,' in *Managing the Global Firm,* eds. Yves Doz, Ghoshal Bartlett and Gunnar Hedlund (New York, London: Routledge, 1990), 363.

Hennart, J. F., *A Theory of Multinational Enterprise* (Ann Arbor: University of Michigan Press, 1982).

Hergert, M. and Morris, D., 'Trends in International Collaborative Agreements' in *Cooperative Strategies,* eds. Farok Contractor and Peter Lorange (Lexington, MA: Lexington Books, 1988), 99–109.

Hirshleifer, J., 'The Private and Social Value of Innovation,' *American Economic Review* (1971), 561–574.

Hladik, Karen J., 'R&D and International Joint Ventures,' in *Cooperative Strategies,* eds. Farok Contractor and Peter Lorange (Lexington, MA: Lexington Books, 1988), 187–204.

Houghton, James R., 'Corning Cultivates Joint Ventures that Endure,' *Planning Review* 18 (September–October 1990), 15–17.

'How to Manage in the White Spaces,' *Supervisory Management,* 39 (December 1994): 6, 10.

Hull, F., Slowinski, G., Wharton, R. and Azumi, K., 'Strategic Partnerships,' in *Cooperative Strategies,* eds. Farok Contractor and Peter Lorange (Lexington, MA: Lexington Books, 1988), 445–456.

'Intel and AT&T Join Forces on Video Telephone,' *New York Times,* August 23, 1994, D4.

Jain, S.C., 'Perspectives on International Strategic Alliances,' in *Advances in International Marketing,* ed. S.T. Cavugril, Vol. 2 (Greenwich, CT: JAI Press, 1987), 103–120.

Jarillo, C.J., 'On Strategic Networks,' *Strategic Management Journal* (January–February 1988), 35.

Jemison, David B. and Sitkin, Sim B., 'Acquisitions: The Process Can Be a Problem,' in Christopher A. Bartlett and Sumantra Ghoshal, *Transnational Management: Text, Cases, and Readings in Cross-border Management* (Homewood, IL: Irwin, 1992), 504.

Kanter, Rosabeth Moss, 'Becoming PALs: Pooling, Allying and Linking Across Companies,' *Academy of Management Executive,* 3, 1989, 183–193.

Kanter, Rosabeth Moss, *The Challenge of Organizational Change* (New York: Free Press, 1992).

Kanter, Rosabeth Moss, *When Giants Learn to Dance: Mastering the Challenge of Strategy, Management, and Careers in the 1990's* (New York: Simon & Schuster, 1989), 115.

Katz, M. and Shapiro, C., 'Network Externalities, Competition, and Compatibility,' *American Economic Review,* 75 (1985), 424–440.

Killing, Peter, 'How to Make a Global Joint Venture Work,' *Harvard Business Review* 60 (May–June 1982), 120–127.

Killing, Peter, *Strategies for Joint Venture Success* (London: Croom Helm, 1988a), 11.

Killing, Peter, 'Understanding Alliances: The Role of Task and Organizational Complexity,' in *Cooperative Strategies,* eds. Farok Contractor and Peter Lorange (Lexington, MA: Lexington Books, 1988b), 57.

Kogut, Bruce, 'Joint Ventures: Theoretical and Empirical Perspectives,' *Strategic Management Journal,* 9 (July–August 1988), 332.

Krubasik, Edward and Lautenschlager, Hartmut, 'Forming Successful Strategic Alliances in High-Tech Business,' in *Collaborating to Compete*, (eds) Joel Bleeke and David Ernst (New York: Wiley, 1993), 60.

Levitt, Theodore, 'The Globalization of Markets,' *Harvard Business Review*, 61 (May–June 1983), 92–102.

Lewis, Jordan D., *Partnerships for Profit* (New York: Free Press, 1990a).

Lewis, Jordan D., 'Using Alliances to Build Market Power,' *Planning Review* (September–October 1990b), 5.

Limerick, David and Cunnington, Bert, *Managing the New Organization* (San Francisco: Jossey-Bass Publishers, 1993).

Lorange, Peter, 'Creating Win-Win Strategies from Joint Ventures,' *The CTC Reporter* (Spring, 1991), 8–12.

Lorange, Peter and Roos, Johan, *Strategic Alliances: Formation, Implementation, and Evolution* (Cambridge, MA: Blackwell Business, 1992), 19.

Lutz, Robert A., 'Implementing Technological Change with Cross-Functional Teams, *Research-Technology Management*, 37 (March–April 1994), 14–18.

Mansell, Robin, *The New Telecommunications* (London: Sage Publications, 1993).

McManus, J., 'The University Connection,' *Enterprise*, 1991, 35–39.

Mintzberg, H., *The Nature of Managerial Work* (New York: Harper & Row, 1973).

Mowery, David C. and Rosenberg, Nathan, *Technology and the Pursuit of Economic Growth* (Cambridge: Cambridge University Press, 1989).

Mytelka, Lynn Krieger, *Strategic Partnerships: States, Firms and International Competition* (Rutherford, NJ: Farleigh Dickinson Press, 1991).

Nohria, Nitin, 'Internal Corporate Venturing at Eastman Kodak: A New Chapter in the Rise and Fall of the New Venture Division' (Cambridge: Harvard Business School, Divsion of Research, *Working Paper*, 92–075), 21.

Nortel Daily Information Service, September 1, 1994; available from Northern Business Information Inc.

Ogilvie, Heather, 'This Old Office,' *Journal of Business Strategy*, 15 (September–October 1994), 26–30.

Ohmae, Kenichi, *Triad Power*, (New York: Free Press, 1985).

Ohmae, Kenichi, 'The Global Logic of Strategic Alliances,' *Harvard Business Review* 67 (March–April 1989); 143–154

Osborne, Richard N. and Baughn, C. Christopher, 'Forms of Interorganizational Governance for Multinational Alliances,' *Columbia Journal of World Business*, 33 (1990); 503–519.

Paap, Jay, 'A Venture Capitalist's Advice for Successful Strategic Alliances,' *Planning Review*, 18 (September–October 1990), 20–22.

Pekar, Peter Jr. and Alio, Robert, 'Making Alliances Work–Guidelines for Success,' *Long Range Planning*, 26 (August 1994), 54–66.

Pfeffer, J. and Nowak, P., 'Joint Ventures and Interorganizational Interdependence,' *Administrative Science Quarterly*, 21, (1978), 398–418.

Pfeffer J. and Salancik, G.R., *The External Control of Organizations* (New York: Harper & Row, 1978).

Porter, Michael, *Competitive Advantage: Creating and Sustaining Superior Performance* (New York: Free Press, 1985).

Porter, Michael, 'From Competitive Advantage to Corporate Strategy,' *Harvard Business Review*, 65 (May–June 1987), 43–59.

Porter, Michael, *The Competitive Advantage of Nations* (New York: Free Press, 1990), 34–35.

Powell, W.W., 'Neither Market nor Hierarchy,' *Research in Organizational Behaviour* (December 1990), 295–366.

Prahalad, C.K. and Hamel, Gary, 'The Core Competence of the Corporation,' *Harvard Business Review*, 3 (May–June 1990), 87.

Primozic, K.I. and Leben, J., *Strategic Choices: Supremacy, Survival, or Sayonara* (New York: McGraw-Hill, 1991).

Rockart, John F. and Bullen, Christine V., 'A Primer on Critical Success Factors' (Cambridge, MA: Center for Information Systems Research, Sloan School of Management, 1991), 64.

Saffo, Paul, 'Business Goes Organic, Menlo Park: Institute for the Future,' *InformationWeek*, January 2, 1985, 3, 7.

Schenker, Jennifer, 'Alliances Face Integration Headache,' *Communications Week International*, July 18, 1994, 26.

Schiemann, William A., 'Organizational Change Start with Strategi Focus,' *Business Strategy*, 14 (January–February 1993), 43–48.

Schoen, Donald, *Technology and Change* (New York: Delacorte Press, 1967).

Shipley, David 'Cross-functional Teams,' *Management Decision*, 32, 17,20.

Shrader, Stephan, 'Informal Technology Transfer Between Companies: Information Leakage or Know-how Trading?,' 1989, Sloan School, *Working Paper*, Dewey Library (Cambridge, MA: MIT).

Sjoberg, Per-Olof, 'The Management of Interfirm Alliances' (MS thesis, MIT, 1992).

Smythe, George, interviewed by Universe (Nashville: Northern Telecom Inc.. Spring 1994), 10.

Snow, T. and Melcior, T., 'Designing a Target Enterprise: Business Modeling at United Technologies Microelectronics Center,' presented at the Dooley Group 10th Annual Executive Conference, December 1991.

Sprague, Ralph H. Jr. and McNurlin, Barbara C., *Information Management Systems in Practice* (New Jersey: Prentice-Hall, 1986), 121–128.

Starbuck, W.H., 'Acting First and Thinking Later: Theory Versus Reality in Strategic Change,' in *Organizational Strategy and Change*, ed. Johannes M. Pennings (San Francisco: Jossey-Bass, 1985), 563.

Stonesifer, Richard J., 'The Boundaryless Company,' The Conference Board, 1993.

Teece, David, J., *The Multinational Corporation and the Resource Cost of International Technology Transfer* (Cambridge: Ballinger, 1976).

The Information Deal Making Directory (Boston: BRP Publications, Inc., 1994).

'The Strategic Partnering Process' (Greenwich, CT: Stockman & Associates), 1991.

Utterback, James M. and Suarez, Fernando, 'Dominant Design Paradigms and the Survival of Firms' (Cambridge: MIT Press, 1991).

White, Roderick, E. and Poynter, Thomas A., 'Organizing for World-wide Advantage,' in *Managing the Global Firm*, eds. Yves Doz, Ghoshal Bartlett and Gunnar Hedlund (London: Routledge, 1990), 95–111.

Bibliography

Williamson, Oliver E., *Markets and Hierarchies: Analysis and Antitrust Im
plications* (New York: The Free Press, 1975), 8.

Williamson, Oliver E., *The Nature of the Firm* (New York: Oxford Univer
sity Press, 1991).

Yost, Matt and Devlin, Kathleen, The State of Corporate Venturing,' *Venture
Capital Journal* 33 (June 1993), 37.

Index